# Being Transparent

## *With Yourself, God, and Others*

Susan M. Sims

ISBN-10: 0989440419

ISBN-13: 978-0-9894404-1-7

"Scripture taken from the NEW AMERICAN STANDARD BIBLE®, Copyright ©1960,1962,1963,1968,1971,1972,1973,1975,1977,1995 by The Lockman Foundation. Used by permission."

This book is dedicated to my husband, Brian. He continually shows me God's love and allows me to live my dream daily by being his wife and the mother of our children. I'll love you for always.

*and*

To our children: Elizabeth, Erica, and David. Even on the hard days, you inspire me to live out my transparency.

# Acknowledgements

To my Wednesday night Bible study group a few years back. You sat through Bible studies with me, allowed me to write my own questions and materials, and showed me how to truly be transparent.

To my Dad for his theological insight and editing. Your insight not only helped with the book, but your understanding of theology shaped who I am today.

To my Mom and Mrs. Carol Anne Eby for their editing advice and Christian example. You both coached me in different ways throughout my life and I am eternally grateful.

To my brother, Jason, who gave up valuable hours answering my questions and gave me the encouragement I needed to move forward in this endeavor. And, to my brother, Stephen, for your many "life" talks throughout the years that helped me think through transparency.

# Contents

*Introduction* ........................................................................................................ 1

What is Transparency? .......................................................................... 3

Mental Transparency and Expectations ......................................... 20

Physical Health and Transparency ................................................... 45

Transparency with God ......................................................................... 68

Transparency with Others ................................................................... 89

Transparency with Love ...................................................................... 111

# Introduction

Transparency is a sensitive subject that requires some very hard choices. Our struggle with transparency comes from past experiences of being hurt, seeing others hurt, and choosing to trust someone and realizing they let us down. With this in mind, our encounters with others are based upon our view of transparency. How much will we open up with others, and is it safe to open up with everyone? What parts of our lives will we share? Will we risk being hurt again? When we reach the point in our lives where we are skeptical of trusting others, we shut down the idea of being accountable and transparent with them. This lack of accountability, though, opens the door for multiple transparency issues.

In our society today, partly due to social media outlets, we can deceive ourselves into thinking we are more transparent than we really are. One problem we can encounter is that we predominately post the good pictures and tell of the good times in our lives. Likewise, we can have a false sense of transparency with others when we only share the "safe" parts of our lives: the parts we can control and the parts we wish others to see. This mask we create can keep others out and leave little room for true transparency.

Busyness in our calendars and schedules can become another obstacle to our pursuit of transparency. Our jobs, taking kids to sports and music lessons, and trying to fit quality time into our family's schedule, can inhibit our time to be transparent. Because we are too tired from our weekly activities, we do not take the time to interact and to be accountable with others and we lose ourselves in the daily duties. We have to be honest and transparent with ourselves of who we are so we will know how to interact with ourselves, God, and others. Through transparency, we will discover God's love and His desires for our lives. Only then can we truly be transparent.

What we need to realize is that many of our questions throughout life, even in specific circumstances, are based on *our* expectations not being met. What are your expectations of your life? What do you expect from your spouse and/or family? What do you expect people to do for you? What do you expect to do for others? What do you expect God to do for you? All these expectations lead us to question when a situation goes differently than what we had planned. When these times of questioning happen to us, we need to step back and be honest and transparent with ourselves, God, and others. What is going on within our very soul will affect every part of our lives; whether we admit to it or not.

As we embark upon this transparency journey, we will discover God's redemptive love in the process. We will learn to love and let go of things along the way. I invite you to join me as we begin our journey on the road to transparency.

# Chapter 1

# What is Transparency?

*Transparent (def):*
*1. permitting the uninterrupted passage of light; clear*
*2. easy to see through, understand, or recognize; obvious*

What is this transparency stuff, anyway? One would think it should be true to its definition and be clear and easy to understand. Being transparent is hard. It does not come easy to most people. Whether it is the past, feeling like an embarrassment, or the circumstances of life engulfing them, people have a hard time, in general, letting others into their lives. So, how can we become better in being transparent with others? I believe it all starts with us. It starts with knowing our own history and life story. Have you ever sat down and thought about your story? What events in your life have made you the person you are today? Are they events of the past or events in your present? Many fail to realize how their life's circumstances can affect their future. Let me share a bit of my history with you as we begin our "transparency" journey.

My life started out simple enough...a preacher's kid! No pressure at all! I always had an expectation of God in my life for as long as I remember and an expectation I would be a Christian. This was not bad. It came from both inside and outside of the church. The Christian life was how it was done. It was a no-brainer. I don't remember life apart from the church when I was younger. Everything seemed a spiritual issue to me as God was always in everything. My parents taught me the importance of living a Christian life through their words, but more importantly, through their actions. Seeing this Christian life lived out daily at home took away any negative feelings I might have associated with this expectation of being a Christian.

One day, when I was in second grade, I went to the church with my dad. I was playing around the church while he was working on his sermon. When I came back to his office, I found him in the sanctuary kneeling at the first pew crying. Now, this was the first time I had seen my dad cry. My dad was crying while praying. It was such an odd sight for me that I asked him why he would cry while praying. I always thought everything about God would be happy. He said he wanted to make sure he was doing everything he needed to do for God and sometimes that included doing things that were not necessarily his first choice. He was being open and transparent with me. In this process, he opened the doors for me to ask more questions in the future.

The future brought a move a few months later to another city. I was numb as to why God would take me away from my friends. I did not like the new church, and I sure didn't have any friends. The people were mean and mistreated my father. The questions started pouring out of me. Why, God? Why would you allow your people to yell at me every time I go to church? I wanted to run away and go back to my "old" home. I wanted to be anywhere but there. But, there I was and there is where I drew more determined to be a "better" Christian than those teaching me at that church. Something did not feel right inside that building.

Have you ever felt that overwhelming sense of evil surrounding you? That feeling that you are being suffocated and you have to get out of there right away? I felt that way at that church around a certain lady. She scared me. She had the face of a Christian, but she was the devil to me. Her eyes bore right through my soul and I knew she wanted me to hate, rebel, and to love evil. I prayed many prayers that I would not run into her as I entered church on those Sundays and Wednesdays. God drew me closer to Him despite all the evil around me.

One Sunday, something was not quite right with me personally. I was drawn to the altar and felt a desire to ask God to be closer to me than I felt He was. I had been saved a few years back and didn't understand this feeling. In all reality I wanted more; more of God in my life. The Holy Spirit was drawing me to Him. I rededicated my life to Him that day and made a pledge that for the rest of my life I would give Him more and more of me each day. I would do so until I was as perfect as I could earthly be, before I met Him face to face. What happened after that day was amazing. That lady didn't scare me anymore. I remember walking past her and smiling as I looked into her eyes. Her power no longer had a hold on me. I was empowered by the Living God. He was now fighting my battles.

The battles didn't stop there, though. Shortly after this experience in my life, we moved again. This time the church seemed more relaxed and not as stiff. But, Satan was still around. I felt more uneasiness. It was that feeling where something was just not right although everything seemed perfect on the outside. It was the happy faces and masks that were hiding the truth underneath; when in fact, some were not being real with God or themselves. Why were they not being transparent? Why couldn't they be who they really were in all circumstances of their lives? I saw how they compartmentalized different aspects of their lives. God was not over all...He was only one part of their lives. I, sadly, learned from them how to compartmentalize my life. I discovered "me" and my more selfish desires.

An argument could be made that this was all about growing up. I was "growing up" according to the non-church world, but I was growing apart from God. This growing apart also began my learning process of the art of masking. I fully understood how to act as expected when I really wanted to act a completely different way. I knew all the "right and appropriate" answers. I learned how to not be transparent. Even through all my struggles during those years, God placed some important people in my life that made a difference for me.

These people were different because they never changed. They were always the same whether I was at their house or saw them at church. They had the same attitudes and reactions in either place. This transparency was profound to me amongst all the other examples I saw in the church every Sunday. God was showing me there was more to being a Christian than just being available to Him on Sundays and Wednesdays. I knew this to be true in what I saw lived out through my parents, but it was now being modeled through other believers. I saw the praying wife living out Proverbs 31. I saw a husband putting his wife before himself when she couldn't do things on her own. These people were being real to God, themselves, and others. Their lives made a big impact on my growing heart and mind.

God placed a desire in my heart during those years to be real and true. But, can it really be that easy? Are our lives simpler the truer we are with ourselves and God? Again, can it really be that easy? Before I could dig in further, it was time to move again. I was so devastated by what God had taken away from me (obviously my perception) that I did not want to accept what He was giving me. As I threw my tantrum, I missed seeing those things He was giving me. I became numb to those around me. I told God I would pretend to be happy so it wouldn't make my dad look bad in front of the congregation. I also decided I wouldn't get personally involved in people's lives because I was afraid God would make us move again and I would lose my friends. So, I wore a mask and hoped for the best. My friendships weren't growing quickly because of my attitude.

That's when it started to hit me. This is not just about God and me; all I do affects others. All I do! Whether through obeying God or committing sins, through activity or non-activity, it all affects others. Here I thought I was the victim and felt sorry for myself when I was hurting others around me by my inaction to befriend them. I discovered the hard way that we are all linked together. We are all God's creation. So, what does this have to do with being transparent? Everything!

## *Transparent: To be or not to be*

Ah! The famous line from Shakespeare's Hamlet, "To be or not to be, that is the question." Was it better for Hamlet to live and go through all of life's struggles, or was it better to die and live in the unknown of death? He had a choice in front of him and he chose to digress with the rest of the audience. We feel his pain, we acknowledge his confusion, and we somehow start to understand a bit more from where he was coming. Hamlet was being transparent. We got him. We felt him.

If most Christians were asked if they are transparent, many would say, "yes". Really, it would seem like a silly question. Most go to church and worship with friends and visitors alike. They are transparent in their love for God and commitment to Christ, in a limited measure, simply by showing up on Sunday mornings. Others might even attend a Sunday School class or small group accountability Bible study. It is here in these groups where more details are revealed about their lives. The struggles their kids are going through, the help they need with parenting, or the lack of sleep they are receiving due to a heavy workload all point to more disclosures.

They, like Hamlet, discuss their pain and confusion as their way of being transparent. However, as believers get involved with small groups, there comes a point of comfortableness. You know the stories of their lives and know the general happenings of their routines. There seems to be less "big" and important things happening as you grow older together. The surprises come fewer and farther between as you understand their outlook on life. You know why they are where they are in life. They understand you and know why you are where you are in life. Somewhere along the way, because you know each other so well, you will not feel the need to share all the small things in your life. This is the point in which transparency has hit a small speed bump. Now, I'm not talking about finding out how Sally went to work and found out someone was making fun of her red shoes or how the dog continually chewed every fabric in the house. I'm talking about the little things in life that slowly eat away at our souls.

The "little things" of work can bring people down, affect their attitudes, and become their undoing. The kids drive their parents crazy, and the parents feel they can't breathe. Perhaps it's the pain from cancer hurting so much that it hinders seeing God in one's life. As Christians, we might see these things as small and not worthy of a prayer request. What do we do at this point? We, like Hamlet, must decide if it is better to be or not to be: transparent. After his digression, Hamlet chose death. When we dismiss the things of life as trivial or not as important compared to what others are facing, we can begin to slowly die inside. This is when the struggle begins. We will have to choose to share a part of our lives we might consider trivial with someone else. This transparency will not only benefit our souls, but it will also benefit those around us who are secretly struggling. Let's look at two different examples of people on their path to transparency.

Jim woke up one morning to realize he didn't know who he had become or what he wanted for his future. He had a plan for his life growing up and what he had before him was not how he thought his life would be. In his estimation, he was a disappointment to himself. Surely he was a disappointment to those around him, not to mention his wife and kids. Jim went to work daily only to feel completely alone and dissatisfied. The longer he went through his daily routines, the more unfulfilled he felt and the more he wondered if he would ever feel alive again.

Twice a week Jim attended church and was also part of a small group. You see, he had been a Christian for as long as he could remember. He grew up in the church. Church was not only something he attended and believed in, but it was a way of life for him. Jim didn't know life without the church. His entire family, likewise, was involved in church and loved God very much. His wife was perfect for him and his children even made wise choices and seemed to get along on most days. On the outside, others would think this family had it all together.

There was only one problem, though. Jim was not content. There was something missing in his life. Although Jim was involved in many of the "right" areas of life, he did not feel connected. He was searching for meaning and purpose in this so-called perfect life. Not knowing where to turn, Jim poured himself into more "good" activities. He continued living life day-to-day. One thing Jim thoroughly enjoyed was his small group. When it came time for his small group, there were many opportunities to hold each other accountable. Major life changes and circumstances were shared during these times together, as people studied the Bible, yet Jim still had a feeling of discontentment each week. How was he to ask for prayer regarding this? It wasn't like he was addicted to something or having "real" struggles in his life. He did not know the source of his discontentment.

Week after week, Jim's group continued to meet and Jim would ask for prayer for the big ticket items: the sicknesses, the job loss of friends, and the problems his kids faced. More or less, though, he rarely asked for prayer for himself. Everything nagging him seemed so trivial. He knew there was a deeper desire to connect, but he felt unaware of where to begin. Week after week Jim tried to be strong and yet he felt weaker and weaker on the inside. He was shutting down and shutting down quickly.

Mary, on the other hand, was a single mom who didn't grow up in the church. Her high school friends invited her to youth activities and she enjoyed her time there on occasions. In the back of her mind, though, Mary never truly felt she fit in at church. Something was missing. She never felt good enough. After growing up and having two kids to support, Mary was at the end of her rope. Her daughter, June, was always getting into trouble. Her son, Michael, was just the opposite, though. He was so quiet that he often was neglected emotionally because Mary had nothing left for him after dealing with his sister. Mary decided they needed to go to church. She definitely was not as involved as Jim. She participated in the service as a spectator and joined a ladies' small group so she could have some adult time in her life away from the kids.

At first, Mary felt very self-conscious about her circumstances. She didn't think anyone would understand. In all honesty, she was there for selfish reasons: much needed alone time. She had attended the Bible study for three weeks when things began to unravel. It was a rough car ride that night with hurtful words. Upon arriving at church, her daughter exploded as they were getting out of the car. Mary didn't know if she could take anymore of her life. She held it together and made it to the Bible study. The leader that night decided to start off with prayer requests instead of ending with them. It was like a flood trying to spill out of her and Mary could hold it in no longer. She poured out her heart about her struggles with June. Through many tears and words, Mary became transparent.

She was amazed at the sudden peace that overcame her. The outpouring support through prayer was more than she could have imagined. It did not give her daughter a better attitude that night, but she felt somehow the women's group had her back. Every week, through the ups and downs, at least one person would ask how things were going. She was no longer alone. Sadly, June didn't agree with her mom on many things, but Mary's responses to June improved over the weeks and following months. This enabled Mary to have a better perspective on the situation. She soon realized her need for Christ in her life and invited Him into her heart.

Upon first glance, it might seem Jim and Mary had nothing in common. Their lifestyles were different. Their relationships with God were on two different levels. Jim had always been a Christian and Mary was a babe in Christ. The one thing they had in common, though, was trying to handle their lives on their own. Jim didn't think that the trivial mattered and Mary was unwilling, at first, to share any of her struggles. If people are not careful, they can assume they are mature Christians since they have been a Christian for a long time. This argument seems to make sense because Jim knows more about the Bible and hopefully has had more personal encounters with Christ. If Jim knows so much about the Bible and Christ, why is he unwilling to share even the trivial things? Is Jim embarrassed that under his seemingly perfect life that it is not so perfect?

We are treading on shallow ground here. If we are unwilling to share our thoughts with others, we are not only putting ourselves over God in these areas to figure them out on our own, but we are creating masks to those around us. These masks can become stumbling blocks for our friends, children, or most anyone. These little areas we hide from those around us, in fact, are breeding grounds for Satan to work against our desire for a deeper relationship with God. We hold on to the thoughts of seemingly trivial issues, and it seems the longer we refuse to share with others, we are caught in a trap of not knowing how to share. At this point, we continue to deal with them on our own even longer. It's a vicious cycle. We strive to handle them with God "alone" without bothering anyone, when in reality, I fear, we strive to handle them without God. You see, God did not intend for us to go at this relationship thing alone. Why else would He look at Adam in Genesis and say it was not good for him to be alone? It was at that point God created Eve for Adam.

When we feel others do not need to be bothered with our emotions/problems of the day, we essentially convince ourselves we can or should be able to handle these on our own. Logically, this sounds just about right. God created us to use our common sense, and we are to use what He has given us. Yet, when the common sense doesn't seem to be adding up and we are still struggling, it now becomes a pride issue if we do not want to admit to others we need help. We feel we should be above our problems and promote ourselves to a god status of "problem solver – no help needed". Sadly, though, this new promotion never gives us the peace or satisfaction we need or desire. Jim knew all too well how this felt. For so long he was trying to figure out why he wasn't content instead of opening up about his irritations and allowing others to minister to him.

# What is Transparency?

*"Isolation is the sum total of wretchedness to a man."*
*– Thomas Carlyle*

Satan comes ever so gently to remind us how down we feel. How alone and isolated we feel we are from others. We continually call out to God and yet He seems so far away. These feelings can make us feel more out of control and alienated. If we are not careful, we will try harder to overcome these issues and eventually our circumstances are put on a pedestal as we think about them over and over again. Before we realize it, these simple circumstances have enslaved our hearts and minds, and we have no idea how to break the knots to be freed. We think of our isolation continually. Our lives are becoming darker, less clear; not transparent. We try to think how to make our circumstances better; however, we continue to bury ourselves deeper into unrest.

Let me give you an example. Do you remember learning to tie your shoes? Do you remember the frustration you felt when you didn't get it on the first try? How about the fifteenth try? All you have are two strings that need to be formed into a bow, essentially, a knot. I remember after countless tries, I finally tied it in a knot and stuffed the excess shoelaces into my shoes. No one seemed to notice. I was able to go about my day, and I pretended I had tied my shoes correctly. Did you catch that? I was pretending. The hard part came at night when I was all alone and it was time to untie the knot. The knot had been stretched and pulled so tightly during the day that it became too hard for me to untie and I could not take off my shoes. I had to ask my mom for help in untying my knot simply to take off my shoes.

You see, while pretending to have everything just right, I was able to go about my business. When I was alone, though, I literally had nothing to deal with but a knot. This brings us back to the dilemma of being a Christian and not being transparent. When we are not transparent, we allow knots to come in our lives that become harder

13

and harder to undo the longer we walk around pretending everything is fine. What if I had decided not to ask for help the first night? Besides being unable to change clothes and getting my bed dirty, I would have had even a tighter knot the next day. You see, the longer we go about our lives pretending, or not acknowledging the problems, our knots are simply getting tighter and the struggle to free ourselves becomes more difficult.

Mary's knots became more apparent as she revealed them. For the most part, she knew her life wasn't great. She didn't realize what a stronghold these secrets were creating. Her life was new in Christ, so she was still learning how to lean on God for wisdom, strength, and understanding. Jim, on the other hand, did not have any apparent knots. Sure, he had the daily irritations, but it wasn't anything that was huge in his eyes or most others'. Yet, Mary was the one who ended up with the greater peace after opening up and sharing her struggles. Where does this leave the more mature Christian? Where do we draw the line between the things that seem ridiculously simple in our lives that drive us crazy on an almost daily basis and those things that are truly catastrophic in impacting our lives? This is where transparency emerges the winner in both scenarios! If transparency is such a winner, why do most Christians struggle with this issue? I think most Christians truly feel they are being transparent. Well, transparent enough, that is.

> *"We have to distrust each other.*
> *It is our only defense against betrayal."*
> *- Tennessee Williams*

Let's take a walk back to elementary school. You and your two best friends would play on the playground during recess. You knew everything about each other. Then, along came the new kid. You all decided to befriend Sam. It wasn't quite the same with four in the group, but you were able to make it work. Before you knew it, your friends and Sam were hanging out and getting closer by the day. You felt a little hurt because you started to not feel part of the group. What happened next, though, really caused the pain. You found out all the kids had a sleepover at Sam's house over the weekend and you weren't invited. As if this wasn't bad enough, your friends told Sam your deepest, darkest secret that a third grader could have. Not only did this hurt cause you to leave your current friends, but your trust level in friendships just went down a bit.

Middle school came along. You were doing fine with your group of friends. Sam was no longer a concern of yours, but there was Heidi. Heidi was into sports and band like you were. She got you. She understood what made you tick and what made you laugh. You could relax around her more than any others. On your field trip in eighth grade, you began to talk about your future and the latest guy-crush. You noticed Heidi was getting quieter the more you talked. When you asked what was wrong, you realized Heidi liked the same person. How could this happen? But when Billy came up to the two of you and talked only to you, Heidi was infuriated. The next thing you knew she told everyone including Billy about your crush. You were very embarrassed.

I could give you more examples about high school, but I fear the pages could not hold all of the stories. Let's not even talk about college. You see, the older we get, the more jaded and less trusting we become. We realize there are people out there who can and will use our deepest, darkest secrets against us. Why would we want to make ourselves vulnerable to those around us only for them to use it against us? This is the logical conclusion we use in our heads when we tell ourselves that God created us to use common sense, and common sense is telling us to not open our mouths and tell others what we really feel! Where do we go from here?

# What is Transparency?

*"No one can make you feel inferior without your consent."*
*–Eleanor Roosevelt*

How are we supposed to make the leap from using our common sense to opening up to others around us? It comes down to several issues. One I would like to explore right now is trust. How can we truly trust people when we have been hurt in the past? We tend to look at those around us, wonder what their agenda might be, and if we should share our story with them; essentially, our lives. We all have had friendships in which we invested our time and energy only for them to leave us for the next, best friendship. Or, maybe we decide someone knows too much about us and we leave the relationship ourselves before we can get hurt. Either way, after this cycle repeats itself several times, we finally give up and wonder why we would expend more energy. We reason it would be easier to be alone than to try again.

Isolation, though, is not how God intended for us to live. Beginning in Genesis, His desire was a relationship with Him and for us to be companions to one another. Genesis 2:18 states, "Then the LORD God said, 'It is not good for the man to be alone; I will make him a helper suitable for him.'" I like the idea of "suitable for him". This gives me a certain peace knowing that God knows exactly who is suitable for me. Outside of marriage, I may need to share only certain parts of my life story with one person and other parts with another. I don't need to share every dark secret with every person in order to be transparent. However, there is someone or some group of people suitable just for me and who I am. Likewise, there are others out there to whom we are their "suitable helper". Taking this information to heart can only mean one thing: we are to be accountable. We are to be accountable to ourselves, God, and others.

Being accountable takes a lot of trust. Learning to trust and how much trust to place in specific people will involve prayer. Remember, God made individuals, and even a group, suitable for each one of us. We must work to find those individuals or that group. Also, we must be willing to be transparent, as well as, allow others to be transparent with us. Furthermore, we must remember, others are putting their trust in us. Their trusting us is a great honor and must be taken seriously. If we do not have a person or group to begin to share our lives with, we can begin by being transparent to ourselves and God, while He is preparing us for others.

In order to share our lives with others, we need to know something about ourselves first. We are on a journey to discover the person God created us to be. This includes how we look, think, and what expectations we have of our lives. God did a great job creating us. Are we content with how He made us? We all have expectations of our lives. Do these expectations line up with the purpose God has for us? Speaking of God, He is to be trusted with our lives, hopes, and dreams. To the degree we struggle with trusting God with our lives, hopes, and dreams, we will struggle to be transparent. How do you really feel about God being in charge of you? You must realize that only through Him can you find the happiness and contentment that comes from being transparent.

Now, let's dig into our lives a bit to discover the freeing power of being transparent.

## Questions:

1. In what areas of my life am I easily transparent?

2. In what areas of my life do I struggle with transparency?

3. With whom do I struggle the most to be transparent? Me? God? Others?

4. Do you know and accept the story of your life? Are you willing to see yourself as you really are?

5. How has your life story impacted your ability or inability to be transparent in your daily life?

6. What events in your life have made you the person you are today?

7. Write your life story below or on a separate sheet of paper.

### Group Transparency Exercise.

Whether your life's story is more like Jim or Mary's, in your next group prayer time, have every group participant give a personal prayer request. The context of each request should reveal a personal weakness or need, as well as, how God might answer their prayer to help them.

*Chapter 2*

# Mental Transparency and Expectations

Mother Teresa said, "If each of us would only sweep our own doorstep, the whole world would be clean." In the previous chapter, we learned being transparent begins with us, at our own doorstep, by knowing our own story. However, being transparent is more than a one-time cleaning. Being transparent has to become a series of acts that creates a new habit for daily living. When we begin this journey, we may feel lost and immobile, but we must begin.

How do we convince ourselves mentally that it's safe to move forward and be transparent? The mind is a complex being and is screaming "danger" at the thought of being transparent. One danger sign reads, "It didn't work last time; don't open up." Another sign reads, "We've been hurt in the past; don't trust." That little word "trust" involves more than others. We have to get to the point where we can trust ourselves before we expect others to trust us. This is especially difficult for some people.

By knowing our story, we can begin to trust ourselves and know who we are in God. Through the discovery of our story, we then acknowledge some of the expectations in our lives. Throughout life, things can come at us quickly and, if we are not careful, we will make our decisions hastily and not ask ourselves how it will affect us or others. If we do not fully know ourselves, or what we believe, we will not be able to make solid, informed decisions. This, again, reiterates the importance of knowing our story and realizing the impact it has on our lives. This involves a certain amount of accountability and transparency. To be accountable with ourselves seems simple enough, but how is this accomplished?

One form of accountability is setting annual goals. I grew up hearing people talking about losing weight or paying off their debts. Still others promised they would engage more fully with their family and friends rather than simply with work. All these goals seemed great, but I wondered why these same people often complained of not accomplishing last year's goals if these were truly their expectations. I realized it wasn't possible to accidentally overlook a goal if it was written down on paper. My goals were written down that year, and my journey of annual goals began. This goal-writing became part of my pursuit of accountability as it made me aware of my mental expectations in my life.

*"In absence of clearly defined goals, we become strangely loyal to performing daily acts of trivia."*
*–Author Unknown*

Every year as I review my goals, I write a critique of the year including what expectations were met and how my life in general affected my goals and me throughout the year. Again, this accountability has been my attempt at being transparent. Part of the goal process for me is to look over my yearly goals each month to assess how I'm doing with completing the goals. This monthly assessment allows for further transparency regarding whether a goal is still a valid aspiration. For the goals I have completed, I will write down the completion date and mark it off my list. For those yet to be completed, I determine which one I want to accomplish next and work it into my schedule. These goals are written into my monthly, weekly, and even daily schedules to become a reality. After all, these goals have now become an expectation in my life that I want to see completed.

Unfortunately, I don't always succeed with my goals. One year, in fact, only fifty percent of the goals were completed. Upon further review of my goals, I found a quarter of them were unattainable in the timeframe I had allowed. Others, I admitted defeat halfway through the year. The strange fact of my so-called accountability practice concerning my goals is this: nothing happens when I cheat on my goal and it goes unmet. There are no consequences when I don't want to work as hard, and I decide to give myself a little more room to backslide. No one holds me accountable. Overall, it's easier to cheat on my goals or go easy on myself when no one else knows my goals. My system works well for the goals I complete, but not so much for those not completed. I don't typically show anyone else these goals. My goal process is great for accountability with me. It reveals my expectations of life and helps to shape my focus, but the transparency ends with me.

Another form of accountability is sharing our struggles and lives with others. I've told my husband my goals, if he asks, but it's not something hanging up on the wall. This has been a flaw in my system. So, what happens to those goals I really want to do but just get tired of doing in the process? Those are the goals that have stayed on my list for three to four years. In those areas I have not had much progress. In the case of my homemade headboard, taking three to four years to complete the goal was not much of a problem. In the case of doing better with my diabetes and blood sugars, on the other hand, I needed more accountability. Not much harm without a headboard; bad blood sugars over three to four years, though, can do some damage.

Let me explain without all the medical wordage. Having high blood sugar in diabetics is a result of not having enough insulin in their bodies. If there is not enough insulin, the body can't use the sugar for fuel. If the body can't use this sugar for fuel, it will start to break down fats. You might think this is a good thing, but this process actually causes a waste product to be formed that can trigger a diabetic coma. So, how does this apply to being transparent? Well, not telling someone about an incomplete headboard probably won't really matter. But if you have an issue that is like an "elevated" blood sugar, it will eventually cause some damage.

Allow me to share a personal example. One day I took my kids to the park for soccer practice. During this hourly practice, I decided to walk the trails to get some exercise. I checked my blood sugar before walking and all was well. After twenty minutes, I finally reached my favorite part of the trail. This part was completely isolated. You could only see the trees, grass, and trails. No one else was around. There was a bench in the distance and I realized it seemed suddenly far away. My feet weren't acting right. I knew something was wrong with my blood sugar. I couldn't get to the bench quickly enough. Finally, I made it and realized I was in bad shape. I tried to remedy the situation on my own to no avail. Thankfully, someone walked the same trail I enjoyed and helped me. I only received the help I needed because I was willing to be transparent and accountable to someone else. This transparency of our weaknesses, or accountability, is a hard thing to admit to others.

Now, let's go back to Mary and Jim. Mary's spiritual high blood sugars came from her daughter. The high blood sugar was not constant. Since Mary's perspective had changed, mainly due to her transparency, she had more good days than bad. On her bad days, though, the insulin that brought the high blood sugars back down came from her small group where she would pour out her heart. Jim's blood sugars, on the other hand, were elevated due to work situations. None of them were truly related, but they were in fact more frustrating to him than anything else in his life. He never mentioned this to anyone because there was nothing he felt they could do to rectify the situation. So, his blood sugar continued to be elevated as he tried to deal with it on his own. High blood sugars from time to time are not a big deal, but if they are consistent on a daily basis, the waste products begin. Overtime, Jim's body began producing waste products of irritability, impatience, and numbness. He was entering into a spiritual coma and no longer functioning properly. His other waste product was his inability to trust others with his problems.

Trust is a mental road block we must overcome in our journey to transparency. Camillo DiCavour said, "The man who trusts men will make fewer mistakes than he who distrusts them." This is a great quote by human standards, but we believe in more than human standards. Mary trusted others and progressed much further than Jim, who chose not to trust. We, too, must be willing to trust others, but we are to put our trust in God. Proverbs 3:5 states, "Trust in the LORD with all your heart and do not lean on your own understanding." We have a lot more security in trusting God than trusting others. If we are hurt by others, our minds will send us the "danger" signs telling us not to trust. How are we to get from one point of being hurt, past the danger signs, and to the next step of trusting? It has to come from God. He is the only One in Whom our trust can be made whole in this process of becoming transparent.

There is a lot of distrust in our world. We, at times, have unfortunately been on the receiving end of this distrust and, at other times, we have generated this distrust. We, also, have blamed others rather than trusting them. We may think we understand where others are coming from and may believe we can't entrust ourselves to them, but we must realize "others" do not represent everyone. Since some can be trusted, we must acknowledge hiding within ourselves is not the only option. We also have the option to come out of our isolation. The question is, when we come out of our isolation and begin to trust others, what takes place deep within us?

To be able to share ourselves with others requires some introspection. This introspection is another hurdle to overcome in transparency. We cannot pretend to have it all together. We have to be transparent with ourselves to truly understand why we are the way we are and why we react the way we do in certain situations. Are we frustrated because it's time to move in a different direction with our lives? Are we mad because there needs to be justice brought to a situation? There are times during this introspection we will not want to focus on ourselves and our expectations. If we were to focus on ourselves, we might learn we are disappointed in ourselves or in our lives. This questioning of ourselves takes a lot of courage. The questions we ask of ourselves will be different from what others ask; yet, we must proceed with the questioning if we want to truly be transparent.

Like Jim, we may feel we have failed if we are not content with our lives. We ask the questions in order to be transparent and we still feel confused at how to fix ourselves. Ultimately, we grow tired of the introspection and shift our focus to someone or something else. It's easier for us to solve someone else's problem. This is merely a distraction for us in the transparency process. All the while, our discontentment continues to grow because we are not getting at the root of our problem and/or discontentment. The daily routines will become a chore to us and our "blood sugar", like Jim's, will continually be elevated. We must stay on task, though, and ask the questions in order to understand ourselves and our problems. Unfortunately, we don't always have the proper perspective on our problems.

Let's think of our perspective in terms of a puzzle. We know what a puzzle should look like when we see the picture on the box. But what happens when the picture is not on the box? We start with what seems the easiest. We group the blue pieces together to create the sky and the puzzle begins to take shape. Moving forward we have two choices. One, we can get frustrated when certain pieces cannot be found or other blue pieces do not seem to fit anywhere; ultimately, perceiving this as a problem. Or, two, we might just live in the moment of completing the sky until we suddenly realize the picture now has the tops of mountains forming and we become aware of a bigger picture forming.

Our lives are like this puzzle. We can only see a small portion of the puzzle and not the completed one. God is holding the top of the box with the full picture. We take the pieces He has placed in front of us and begin putting them together one by one. Our view is limited without God's help, and we must trust His perfect will. After we complete the sky of our puzzles, we look to see what part to complete next. When reviewing the puzzle, it doesn't make sense unfinished because it is still incomplete. Our deep introspection within, though, requires us to remember the bigger picture and acknowledge our expectations. What do we expect out of this puzzle of life? Will we choose the first option above and be frustrated with our limited view of this smaller section knowing we cannot do this thing called life on our own? Or, will we live in the moment and allow God to show us His expectations of our lives, the mountains coming into view, one piece at a time?

Whether Jim or Mary's lives had turned out as they originally planned, one thing they had in common was certain expectations of their lives. Likewise, we all have some expectations of our lives. It could be as simple as expecting the electricity to work when we flip the switch or expecting our car to run when we get ready to leave the house. You could expect your spouse will keep the vows you made to each other on your wedding day. If you have children, it could be an expectation they will do certain jobs around the house. You might expect to have a job until you retire. These are our mental expectations of us, our family, and life. If we want these expectations to be realized, we must communicate in such a way that they are clear. In order to truly be transparent with ourselves, we must not only be clear on our expectations, we must consider if they are attainable, either for ourselves, or others. Again, we can only discover this answer by taking an even deeper look inside of ourselves.

We were all young and innocent once. Whether you were a girl who believed in happily ever after or a young boy who would brave the world to take care of his bride, we all had dreams and expectations of what we thought our lives would be like one day. Do you remember your dreams of what you thought life would be like when you were older? How does this compare with your life today? Are you disappointed? Do you wonder over and over again if you could have done better somehow? If we are honest, I believe we could all say we could have done some things better. The real question is, "Are you content with where you have landed?"

This is where it hits the hardest for me. Contentment is not a simple question and answer. Contentment is more about asking the question, "Do I trust God enough with my life so that whatever circumstances I am in I can fully rely upon Him for my heart's desires? Ultimately, am I satisfied where I am?" I'm not sure I completely trust

God with my life. At times, without realizing I do this, I live my life believing I could do better with my life and do better at fulfilling my desires than God could do for me. I take my focus off God and put my focus on me and my selfish desires.

God constantly reminds me what my focus is during my devotions. My prayer journals, through the years, have truly shown what was important to me at different times in my life simply by looking at what was being prayed. My expectations were clear by my prayers and how I prayed those prayers. The times I prayed for God's will to be done were the prayers that seemed to be answered more quickly. At others times, when I was worried how a certain situation was going to affect me, those prayers were not answered at all as I had prayed. In both instances, I thought my expectations of the specific circumstances were set correctly. I had been having my devotions regularly, if not daily. I was praying for God to work in the situation and yet nothing was happening.

Then I had one of those moments that could only come from God. I realized I was only worried about me. I was not worried about God getting glory in any of my prayers. It was all about me. This hurt. I knew I had disappointed God and what He wanted for me in my life. My head knowledge was telling me I loved God more than my life, but my actions didn't line up with my thinking. The reality, though, was I was not living out my Christian life as if I believed that statement. Instead of living a trusting and worry-free life, I fretted over what "could be" and the "what ifs". I was not being transparent with God.

I was disappointed with myself at this point and in a bit of shock. I was a pastor's daughter who should know better! I had the knowledge of who God was and what He was, but I forgot the importance of who God was as God Himself. I was ultimately forgetting to allow God to control my mind, thoughts, ideas, dreams, and expectations. I was trying to be god over my mind, thoughts, ideas, dreams, and expectations; forget about transparency.

Have you ever struggled with a certain issue in your life where you were determined you could get over it on your own? You worked day in and day out to get it under control only to come up empty-handed. You asked yourself multiple times what you did wrong. Then, you began to pray and beg God for understanding as to why this was not working out for you. God then reminded you through His word in Proverbs 23:7a, "For as he thinks within himself, so he is." The truth is, the way we think can lead us down the right path or the wrong path.

We continue to ask God to help us get through our circumstances. God then reminds us that we're not asking for Him to walk through our problems with us or to take our problems upon Himself. We are ultimately asking God to give us the strength to do it on our own. Mentally, we are not letting go! This must sound absurd to think we ask God to give us strength to deal with life's burdens in order to give us glory. I definitely do not go around thinking this as I pray, but I can read it between the lines of my journals.

I understood this struggle of burdens more clearly as my husband, kids, and I were cleaning out our garage and cars one day. There were two big garbage bags of clothes that were given to us in the back of our van. I asked our youngest if he would take them inside for me. He wasn't too happy with the request. The next thing I know, I see him struggling and grunting to get both bags inside at the same time. I had not told him he had to get them in at the same time. I simply stated he needed to take them into the house. But, because he did not want to take them inside, he decided to get it done as quickly as possible. The problem with this plan, though, was he made it more difficult than it had to be. It was interesting to me that due to the weight of both bags he had to walk very slowly. So, in retrospect, he could have carried one bag at a time, made two trips, and still completed the task in the same amount of time it took him to carry both bags at once.

How often do I do the same thing with what God asks of me? Too many times, I'm afraid to admit! God will ask something of me and, because I really don't want to do the task, I will complete it as quickly as possible in my mind. I usually make it harder than it has to be, and I am miserable in the process. I struggle with the two bags, walking slowly and grunting in the process. I am complaining in my mind because this is not part of my expectations for the day, just as I'm sure my son was doing at that time. All the while, God is seemingly sitting in the van, cleaning the windows, and wondering why I chose to make a simple task so difficult.

So, the question becomes, how much do I expect of myself in a certain circumstance and how much do I expect God to handle? I always enjoy the small things. I can handle those; at least, a couple at a time. It's when life throws about ten of them at me at once that I feel the pressure. This is the time I feel really spiritual and transparent with God because this is when I go to God and ask for help. I know I can't make it on my own. My expectation tends to be that God needs to bail me out of my overwhelming circumstances, and I'll get the small stuff. Does God really need to be bothered with the small stuff?

I still struggle with the following dilemma: I expect for me, as a highly-educated individual, to have some common sense and to be able to get myself through some certain circumstances. I don't expect to have to rely upon someone or something else. I should be able to get my job done even when I'm overwhelmed with life's circumstances, so why would I ask God? I just do my job! My husband says that I should tell him and/or the kids when I'm feeling overwhelmed so they can help me. If my husband asks this of me, why wouldn't my next logical step be to ask God for help? Both my family and God are on my team. My problem with asking for help comes from a deeper issue and one that is a detriment to truly being transparent: pride.

I never thought I would struggle with pride because of what I wanted to do with my life. My expectation of my life as a little girl was to be a wife and a mom. My mother was able to stay at home with us when we were children, and I loved having my mom at home. With moving so many times while I was younger, there was security in knowing I had family. I wanted that security for my kids. I wanted to be a housewife who made clothes for her children and cooked for the family. Our lives would be just like "Little House on the Prairie"! What do I do now? I stay at home, make some clothes for the kids, and cook. I do the laundry, sew on buttons, buy groceries, help at school, and provide a loving home environment. It appears I should be completely content with the dream God has allowed me to live out daily.

I view the reality of my situation differently, though, when I help at school in my jeans and t-shirt. The working professional mom is there and says, "Oh, you could do such a great job with your skills and could get paid." I then realize I'm nothing to this world. I mean, really, I stay at home. I don't get paid for what I do, and my husband gets up every day to make a living for us. Who notices me except for my husband and kids? I feel so small compared to others. I begin to retreat within myself. This is when I want more. My selfish tendencies emerge. I want more attention. I want more of me. Ugh…there IS my pride. Where do all these feelings come from? Why do I allow others' views of life to interfere with my ultimate goals? I thought all of my expectations were being met?

> *"There are many of us that are willing to do great things*
> *for the Lord, but few of us are willing to do little*
> *things."*
> *– D.L. Moody*

My expectations were being met. The little things I did were little because I did not feel important enough in others' eyes. How do you express to someone your desire of more attention or more self-worth? I have found the more I try to hide my life and feelings from others, and not be transparent, the more questions I tend to have of my life and how I live. I wonder how many times I've said something or acted out before thinking and am confused at my reaction. Why do these certain words or actions surprise me? We try to filter parts of our lives so others will see us in a certain light. Could it be that we have worn a mask so long so others cannot see us, that we have even fooled ourselves? No wonder we become surprised at what we say and how we act.

Beneath these questions is a more important one; what do we think about the most? Again, Proverbs 23:7a reminds us, "For as he thinks within himself, so he is." So, what do we think about the most? What keeps us up at night? What do we spend most of our time mulling over? Do we realize a person is who they are in their leisure more than in their labor? Yes, this is who we really are whether we admit it or not! These things that we think about, worry about, struggle over, and make plans about are deeply important to us. In part, these represent our expectations of ourselves and potentially our lives.

"As he thinks within himself" includes worry. If we tend to worry to the point we can't get something out of our minds, does this mean we are not a trusting person? Would we really rather do it all on our own instead of simply handing something over to God? Do we ever take the time to dig deeper to discover the origins of how we think and what we think about? Do we bring something else into our lives to help us mask the pain of the unknown? Are we too lazy to deal with our insecurities, or just too plain tired to try to find the time to deal with any issue we might have in life? I believe we have to be transparent with ourselves mentally to be able to reach down in the depth of our soul and dig out the roots of the thorns which so easily entangle through our very lives. We have to make our dirt worthy of a good and proper plant. Are you ready to get dirty?

In order to plant our good and proper plant, we will first put on a set of work gloves. Although we know we will get dirty, we will want a form of protection for our hands as we begin to dig deep into the unknown. So it is when we begin to be transparent with ourselves and look at our own lives. We begin with protection. We put up barriers and walls to protect ourselves from hurts that might come along the way. Our walls will help "mask" the pain if anything gets too personal. Have you ever told yourself, "Aw, it's not as bad as you might think it is; cut yourself some slack; you've had a really hard week"? Have you ever tried to say something is not quite as bad as it seems so you will have to work less to resolve the issue?

Let's continue on with the example of our plant. We have the gloves on and are digging deep within the soil. We realize there are bugs living in the dirt. There are only two bugs in the hole you've dug. Not bad, you think, but you're afraid they might eat the roots of your plant. So, you have two options. One, you can go back to the hardware store and buy some bug killer and then finish planting the plant a few days later. The only problem with this is you will get dirty again. The second option is to just plant your plant and hope for the best. In this last scenario, you will be done and will not have to get dirty a second time. Let's look at the two outcomes. In the first option, you have a healthy plant that took longer to get in the ground due to taking care of the bugs before planting. The second option leaves you with a less than perfect plant longing for better soil. How does this apply to being transparent?

We are the soil. We can read of the parable of the sower and the seed in three different gospels: Matthew, Mark, and Luke. How the seed grew depended upon the soil upon which it landed. Jesus gives us the parable of the soil for a reason. It is up to us to produce the kind of soil needed for our lives. When troubles or hard times come, how do we handle what's going on? I believe it starts in our minds with our beliefs. So much of what we do is based on our beliefs. Do we really know in what or Whom we believe? Knowing what or Whom we believe in and owning those beliefs, whether good or bad, is essential as we become mentally transparent.

How can we as mere humans be transparent with ourselves? One place would be to use common sense. Common sense tells us far more than what we usually want to hear and is needed for both spiritual and non-spiritual issues. Unless God specifically tells us what to do, we need to use a measure of common sense in determining how transparent we are to become. Common sense is not only a tool to use concerning transparency; it can be a window showing the work through which we can see ourselves and others.

Let's go back to the plant and the soil with bugs. In the first scenario, you decide it's too hot outside; you're already sweaty and there's rain in the forecast for the rest of the week. You're nasty and gross from kneeling in the dirt and have no desire to repeat this day again. You think, "I really don't want to deal with this plant next weekend, so let's get it in the ground now and be done with it." It looks great the first week because of all the rain. You are so proud of the work you've done and how you got it done quickly. Then, two weeks go by and you notice some yellowing and wilting. Seriously? You worked so hard to get it in the ground.

You remember how hot that day was and how long it took you to get cleaned up after you were done. You are mad that it all seems a waste of time and effort. Are you mad at the plant? Do you blame the sun, the dirt, or yourself? What prompts us to plant without killing the bugs? I think logically we know the bugs should have been killed first before planting. This would put the blame on us for planting without properly preparing the soil. But, does taking care of inconveniences take too much effort? For many of us it does. We want it done now. We are the "fast food" society and we want it immediately.

Sadly, though, I think there's nothing worse than going through a hard time of planting to then have the plant die. These are like the times we decide we will go all in and be transparent to only find ourselves hurt and frustrated. It's so irritating to go through all the work to get through a trying time for it to amount to nothing and all efforts have to start over again. I usually regret my hurriedness at that point. I was working in my garden this spring and preparing the soil. I had removed what I could see to be bad for the plants and was getting ready to plant the seeds. I decided to till the soil a little more when I hit roots. It was the roots of the weeds I had pulled up earlier that week.

I thought I had gotten everything the first time. You couldn't see anything from looking at the garden that would pose a threat, but there it was. It was underground. I fought with those roots for about three minutes. I was so mad. Something snapped inside of me and the tears just came down. God, at that moment, said to me, "This is your life. It looks fine from where you are standing, but I see troubling roots lying underneath. You don't see them, but they have to be uprooted to bring Me glory. They will choke the seeds I'm planting in your life." The reality of my life hurt. Many times I'm so busy doing for others that I forget to take care of me. Or, as I'm busy, I'll pull out what is clearly visible and leave the roots behind.

What roots in your life are choking the seeds God has planted in your life? One root for me, personally, is when an area of my life annoys me. This is usually an area God never desired for me to be involved with in the first place. These are things that appear to be good things, but just do not get me excited when it comes time to do them. I tend to go through a form and do them with little or no emotion. I get one more thing on my plate that takes additional time and I become exhausted. No matter how small the task, if I'm not supposed to be doing it, it becomes my unraveling. I become choked!

Is there something you do on a regular basis and resent it the whole time? Resentment is a second root of my life with which I struggle. For me, these are usually situations I find myself or my family in at a particular time. These situations could include sickness, a tragic accident, loss of a job, or death of a family member or friend. Whatever the situation, the lasting effects change the entire course of my life. I can no longer go back to being who I was before the event and my family dynamics change forever. Through my perspective, I now have a new life.

As I continue to live this life daily, I become embittered and resentful of this change in my life. At this point, God is ready for me to see this "new life" with His eyes, but I'm not always there with Him. We're back to expectations. My expectations of my life are no longer matched up with God's expectations. I am forever trying to figure out my life and where it should go. Remember our puzzle? I don't know what's best for me; God does.

Let's go back to my history. We moved and I had decided I would not allow anyone to get close to me. I knew we would probably move again, and I wanted to avoid getting hurt. I began to protect myself instead of giving myself to God for His use and glory. Little did I know that by my not being open to friendship, I was denying an answered prayer to the one trying to befriend me. She wanted to have a best friend and prayed for one and I, by my selfish stubbornness, was refusing her. She was transparent with me and confronted me one day in tears and asked why I wouldn't befriend her, and my walls broke down instantly. I expected to handle my life better than God.

Life seemed to go along fine for a while and God was shaping me and working in my life. I knew Him mentally and this head knowledge was becoming more of a heart knowledge and a way of life. My life was in line with God's desires for the most part. I dated a very good guy for a couple of years, and we were planning to get married. I thought the puzzle was turning out nicely. It seemed like the mountains were coming into view. I couldn't seem to place my finger on it, though, but deep down I knew something wasn't right. Something about the puzzle was wrong. Three days before Christmas the guy I was dating told me God wanted us to break up and end everything.

The first real emotion I remembered feeling that day was anger. I had a plan for my life. It was as though someone had hit the table and the puzzle was scattered to the ground. I couldn't see the mountaintops anymore. I wondered how my life would ever be the same. These expectations and plans I had for my life were crumbling before me. How could I face my friends and all those who were to be in the wedding? What would people think of me? I was so embarrassed! I was such a failure in my own eyes. I made it all about me. He was doing what God had told him and I was angry at both him and God.

That was a very hard Christmas for me. I woke up on Christmas morning not really feeling much of anything. I remember staring at the ceiling as if I were looking up at God. Tears streamed down my cheeks as I begged God to forgive me that I wasn't happy about today being His birthday. I was so hurt by all that had happened that I literally felt I had nothing to bring to God. I no longer had any expectations of my life. My dreams and plans of what I thought I wanted for my life were all gone. My old dreams were no longer a reality. I wiped my eyes and looked back up at the ceiling and said, "God, I don't know how You could possibly use me, I have nothing to offer You, but please use me if You can." This was the first time I recall being one hundred percent transparent with God. I had nothing to hide from God for He knew all my baggage.

You see, at that moment in my life, my expectations were that I couldn't do anything apart from God. I realized all my ideas, hopes, and dreams were nothing apart from God. Apart from God they were all about me. I was tired of me and wanted Him. This began a great year of learning to lean on God and God alone. Being made in God's greater image became my expectation. I looked to the skies and saw God. I saw Him in the leaves changing colors in the fall. I saw Him at work all around me. He was my expectation. Has God ever been your expectation?

I wish I could say God has always been my expectation, but life gets a little messy at times, and I tend to forget that I'm truly useless without God's guiding and leadership in my life. The next year of my life I acted like Abraham in Genesis 20. God had been so faithful to Abraham and Sarah and proved to them He would provide for them. Yet, when it came time to tell the truth to the king about Sarah being his wife, Abraham lied and told the king Sarah was his sister. I, likewise, saw God's faithfulness, and yet I ran away the next year to a place no one would know me or my past.

I was running from facing my past of disappointment and embarrassment with other people. I decided I could do this life thing on my own with just God and me. A few months later, after what I thought was very successful hiding from others, I met my future husband. He showed me unconditional love and grace. He helped me work through my mental struggles without condemnation. This was an example of when God showed me my expectations of doing things on my own were so below what He intended for me.

Throughout my marriage and life as a wife and mother, many expectations have changed. These expectations not only come from within, but from the world outside. I have the privilege to stay at home with my children. I laugh as I say privilege because there are many days I know it would be easier to go to work and have some time by myself without kids hanging all over me twenty-four hours a day. My expectation of my life is a completely manicured home both on the inside and out and a place of rest and peace. If you could see our home at times, you would know my expectations are far from being met. Many days I hang on just to stay mentally stable. I don't have adult interaction. My house is a wreck. The children are fighting. Oh, the struggles of unmet expectations.

One by one the kids made their way to school and more expectations came. More emptiness was around me, and my expectations somehow increased. I just knew I would have more time to do things I've always wanted to do. But that time never seemed to come like I thought it would. Projects were started but not finished. Not all the beds were made every morning. I felt out of control half of the time, but still I tried to fit more into my schedule. These many years of trying to fill the void and trying to make something of myself (at least in my mind) have sometimes left me tired, cranky and not doing so well. During these transitions in my life, I forgot to readjust my expectations of life.

So, this brings me to the present. God has been speaking to me through my garden, once again. Everything looks great from my kitchen window, but when I get up close and personal I start to see some weeds that might need to be pulled. In a hurry, I reach for the weeds and pull, hoping to get all the roots. It's not until I take the time to tenderly care for the plants that I realize there are roots underneath choking the food and fruit I'm trying to grow. *My roots are the very expectations I have of my life.*

For instance, I expect to get in shape when I exercise and eat right. Likewise, I expect to gain weight and feel bad when I don't. I expect my spouse to be true to only me because he made a vow on our wedding day. Similarly, I expect for me to be true to him as I made that same vow. I expect I should be content everyday when I'm where God wants me to be. Do I live in the moment and allow myself to be content? Or, do I wear myself out with *my* expectations?

I feel sorry for God at times when I think how many times I must have disappointed Him when I thought my expectations were more important that what He had planned for me. Matthew 11:28 states, "Come to Me, all who are weary and heavy-laden, and I will give you rest." God desires for us to come to Him at all times. I love the definition of weary from Merriam-Webster: "exhausted in strength, endurance, vigor, or freshness." The Expositor's Bible Commentary suggests weary as those who have become weary through heavy struggling or toil (Gaebelein 1984, 8:278). Both definitions talk about being tired and both can relate to whatever size the burden may be; whether large or small.

I think we all get and feel this exhaustion in our lives. What makes us this tired? Is it through our struggles, like Mary with her daughter, or through our toils and work, as Jim? Either way, we are to come to God. Do you need help with your endurance of this spiritual race we are running? Are you walking around living a mundane life or are you alive and feeling renewed in your life? We must come to God for rest. This is not limited to physical rest. This rest is mental rest from our "heavy struggling".

Do not miss the fact that we are in multiple mental battles as we travel the road of transparency. We must continually surrender our expectations to God and allow Him to be Lord over our thoughts. Our mental health cannot be overlooked on our journey to be transparent. Verse 30 of Matthew 11 reads, "For My yoke is easy and My burden is light." Before we can end with that verse, though, we must read the meat of the sandwich and study verse 29, "Take My yoke upon you and learn from Me, for I am gentle and humble in heart, and you will find rest for your souls." When we take God's yoke upon us, He then guides us. We move with His direction. My favorite part is "learn from Me". God's Holy Spirit is our teacher. He leads us gently. He shows us how to trust, how to be content, and how to be transparent. Lastly, God gives us rest; rest for our souls. Do you need rest? I do.

You see, God does not ask me to "do" for Him, He simply asks me to "be". He wants me to be nothing more than His child. He is the Father and I am the child. He created me and what He created is good enough. I am to simply love Him. It doesn't matter what this world says about me. I am who God created me to be, and I must be content to be that person. I have to leave my expectations out of the equation. It is not what I think is important, but what is important to God.

But, really, how can we know the difference between what is important to God and what is important to us? We must live an open, transparent life with God. Our lives must be immersed in His words, the Bible, and in open conversations through prayer. In this manner, things that are important to God will be what are important to us. We have to be transparent with ourselves mentally first because God already knows everything about us. It is up to us to admit who we are, what we are doing, and why we are doing what we do. We need to know what we expect and take those requests to God. How can we mentally comprehend that we follow a God who might not have the same expectations for our lives as we have for our lives? We start the plunge into being transparent with ourselves through faith. Perhaps we are doing all the right things. This is great, but we have to continually ask ourselves, through God's Spirit, if what we are doing is God's plan for our lives at that moment in time.

God speaks to each of us in a different way. He desires to be in every part of our lives. Our expectations of life affect how we think, act, and react. We must remember, though, our expectations should not limit God. God desires a relationship with us. Our infinite brain cannot comprehend who God truly is. Isaiah 55:8 states, "'For My thoughts are not your thoughts, nor are your ways My ways,' declares the LORD." He can do much more than we could ever imagine. Likewise, He will not always work in the ways we had planned. Throughout our lives, the one expectation we can always count on is the fact that God will move in our lives if we get out of the way. It's time to move and allow Him to show us the mountains.

## *Questions*

1.  Name three expectations you have for your life?

2.  Are your expectations being met currently, or do you feel unfulfilled?

3.  What expectations of your life did not happen? How does it make you feel to write them down? Relieved? Bitter? Angry?

4.  Do you resent your life or are you content?

5.  What areas of your life bring you joy?

6.  What areas of your life choke and restrict you?

7. Do you feel God has expectations for your life? If so, how do you feel about God's expectations?

8. Is it easy for you to trust God with your life? What makes it hard or easy for you to trust Him?

### Group Transparency Exercise:

Choose one person and give a few moments for everyone to share what they feel God's expectations of that person might be. Do this same exercise with the remaining group members. It might be beneficial to have someone record the expectations of the group.

*Chapter 3*

# Physical Health and Transparency

In the previous chapter, we addressed how the expectations of our lives affect what we do and how we perceive circumstances happening around us. We understand we do not want to limit God as He desires to show us the rest of the puzzle. As we move further along on our transparency journey, we must delve even deeper into this discovery of ourselves through God's eyes. Our physical transparency must start with a clear definition of how we see ourselves and our relationship with our bodies. Once this definition is established, it will influence how we live our lives and how we perceive how the outside world sees us. In this chapter we will look at how this introspective view of ourselves, as well as the view we believe others have of us, pertains to our physical bodies. This inward and outward view of our bodies is linked to transparency, whether in a good or bad light.

Oftentimes, we ignore what life in general can and will do to our bodies. If we do ignore what is happening with our bodies, we will suffer the consequences. God has given us a purpose on this earth. Should we choose to ignore our physical bodies, essentially our health, we are in effect limiting ourselves to do God's work most effectively. Poor health can lead to poor choices and bad attitudes. Poor health, disease, and sickness can also be a result of life even when we try to do all the right things regarding our health. These times must be faced head-to-head with transparency if we are to exhibit God's attitude during our times of testing and hardship. Being a Christian does not negate the fact that our world is a fallen world filled with sin, disease, and struggles. Honest introspection must take place with those affected by disease when their health, or the health of those around them, falls beneath what they expected.

As we live out this journey, we find life happens quickly and, in the process, we have to be certain of who we are in order to make good decisions. We tend to forget and ignore the fact that the physical issues of our bodies affect our lives. Life seems to be going along just fine when one tiny thing happens that changes our lives. It could be something as small as oversleeping because of fatigue and we miss an important meeting, or physically being too tired to adequately finish a project without losing our temper. It could be an illness that will never be cured in our lifetime, or we get a disease that will ultimately take us from this earth. A young child dies unexpectedly. The most common physical things of our health, life, and death, make a difference in our lives. Let's see how the following two people reacted to their given circumstances.

Megan was a well-balanced girl who grew up in a Christian home. She rebelled in her own way, but never gained much attention from those around her. Megan managed to go through life staying out of people's way. She received above average grades at school and landed a good job. Her lifestyle mimicked that of the utmost Christian. Her parents were proud of her and what she had accomplished in her short lifetime. Hard work had taken her to the top of her career. Megan married the man that she had loved since she was twelve, and she volunteered in her church and community. Something was wrong, though, and she wasn't doing well physically.

It started out simple enough with being tired all the time. Megan got to the place where her headaches were numerous. Pain became so intense that it was hard to get out of bed. Muscle soreness was a constant. Pain was never far from her thoughts as it never went away. It wore on her emotionally day in and day out. She went to every doctor possible. For years, no one could tell her what was wrong as all the tests came back negative for a diagnosis. Baffled by all of this, the answer finally came: you need to deal with the stressors in your life. She was confused and asked what exactly this meant. The doctors told her she must evaluate what in her life caused her the most stress. In this manner, she must rid herself of these stressors. None of this seemed to make sense.

Did the doctors have this right, or were they just guessing at a prognosis? Had job stress caused all of this? It wasn't really hard work. Sure, there were some people she wouldn't miss if they left the company, but it wasn't anything she lost sleep over at night. She figured it really couldn't be her job, so she continued working as before. Besides working fulltime, Megan did a lot of volunteer work. This time of volunteering brought a lot of joy and contentment. She enjoyed spending time feeding the homeless at the shelter. While visiting her grandparents in the nursing home on weekends, she would take a couple of hours to help around the nursing home and visit others who didn't have family in town. She knew it was time-consuming to do these extra activities. They were by no means stressful, though. Surely these things she enjoyed couldn't cause enough bodily stress to create this debilitating illness of pain and fatigue.

Slowly, what seemed like a perfect life seemed be to unraveling before her very eyes as her health was slipping through her hands. Everything felt completely out of control and far from her grasp. With her pain and headaches a constant, the little "tasks" in life were becoming a true "chore". The job she loved and the volunteer work she enjoyed were becoming an inconvenience and a bother. Her joy was disappearing slowly, and she began to go through the motions. She became angry at her husband and family because she felt they didn't understand. Not being able to handle her body and life was just an embarrassment to Megan. Determined she wasn't going to change all the good she was doing in life and view herself as a failure, she continued with her job and volunteer activities. Meanwhile, she was becoming numb to everything around her and didn't know how to break the cycle of numbness.

Ron, on the other hand, was fresh out of college with no idea of what he wanted to do or who he wanted to be in life. His great uncle, who raised him, recently died. He was the only family Ron knew. In the will, he found out about a hotel his uncle left him. There was one stipulation, though. Ron could not sell the place until after it was opened for business and in good working order. He had a year to complete the repairs and finalize the grand reopening. It wasn't as though he had anything better to do, so Ron decided to tackle this project.

Unfortunately, this hotel was not like anything he had ever seen before. It was in a decent part of town, but the interior of the building itself was definitely run down. Ron wondered why his uncle never mentioned this place before. His uncle did not leave him a lot of money, and he personally did not have the finances to afford someone to clean it for him if he was going to make all the repairs. He decided he would do the best he could with what he had. He thought it would be best to start with the doorway since it was the entrance. He couldn't believe it! The doorway alone took an entire week to clean. He started to wonder if this hotel was more of a blessing or a curse. It was a slow, drawn-out process. Once inside the cleaned entrance, he looked around for his next task.

The main hallway was the next logical place to continue. Upon further inspection, Ron noticed the wood flooring was warped. He literally had to take boards out one by one. There were times he thought he could not possibly go on as it was extremely painful and the labor was hard. The grand opening was now eleven months away. Frustration set in, as the process was taking longer than expected, when he met a guy who was a flooring expert. He offered to help Ron after work for free because he loved doing floors and had some time on his hands. The flooring job that seemed insurmountable to Ron alone was completed in just one month. He stood back in amazement at the stark difference two months had made. Ron found an old chair, dusted it off, and placed it in the hallway. He sat down and admired the flooring almost forgetting how far he still had to go.

Ron's friend could no longer help as his job took him to another town. Ron was alone again. There were walls that needed repairing, lights to be changed, and painting to be done; not to mention, other flooring jobs to be completed. He wondered how he would do it all on his own. It must have been some sick joke his great uncle had in leaving this place to him. Was his uncle that negligent in overseeing this place before he left it to Ron or had it recently been purchased?

Defeated, he headed to the kitchen. After looking over the area, reality continued to set in of how much more he had to complete and how much work the oven and refrigerator needed. Unfortunately, the oven was not self-cleaning and Ron was forced to scrub away. It was painful. Ron wondered why it had not been cleaned before now. Just thinking of cooking something in this oven should have been a health risk for anyone involved! Ron started to give up and decided it would be better just to buy another one. He sadly realized he couldn't afford a new oven, so he continued scrubbing.

Ron cared about what the hotel looked like. Others came along and tried to influence him to do things differently, but Ron remembered how his uncle liked things and wanted to honor his uncle. He realized, as the owner, it was up to him to keep it clean and continued doing the manual labor. He worked, cleaned, and scrubbed until he was exhausted. This was not at all what Ron imagined being an owner would be. He was working constantly and at the same time, he was feeling a sense of fulfillment inside of himself. Through his constant cleaning, Ron was all too aware of how dirty his hotel was. He was spending countless hours fixing up the hotel so others would be impressed.

The full year passed and the hotel was in business. Although the repairs had been painful, Ron was not ashamed of the place as he once had been. Overall, he knew he did the best with what he had and his efforts weren't in vain. There were plenty of mistakes he had made along the way. If you looked closely, you could see them, but they were not noticeable to others. The places he loved most were the areas he could have glossed over and not fixed, but he chose to fix them. No one would have noticed the cobwebs under the chairs or couches, but he knew they were gone. The closets had been painted and cleaned instead of junk hiding their walls. It was a good feeling to know he had put so much effort into this place. He desired for the outside and the inside to look the same...clean.

Upon review of Megan and Ron's story, Megan struggled to not lose control over her situation while Ron struggled through his situation and achieved a completed hotel. Megan's pain was caused by her busy lifestyle. Due to her refusal to give up her lifestyle or activities, she had pain in her life. Her daily pattern of activities continued regardless of the pain. This only accomplished achieving the same result: pain and frustration. Ron, on the other hand, worked hard to complete a task that was set before him and he succeeded. He was emotionally involved and yet, with a lot of hard work, he completed the task at hand. He had pain and frustration in his process, too, but he continued to move furniture around and clean out the closets. He worked to make a difference.

God has provided a hotel for us in our physical bodies. Our bodies, like Ron's hotel and Megan's lifestyle, are less than perfect. We can either react like Megan or like Ron in our lives. Will we live with the pain and allow it to cripple us, or will we work through the pain and allow God to use our "work in progress" to bring Him glory? Megan's body began to shut down as she continued on her vicious cycle of going through the motions and doing her activities. By not dealing with the stress in her life, and the plain busyness, she was continuing to get her "hotel" cluttered and disorganized and she was becoming ineffective to those around her. Although the outward appearance of Ron's hotel passed the test, he still had to clean the inside in order for it to be a functioning business. Likewise, we must clean our hotels for them to function properly.

Ron realized his hotel was dirty upon walking inside. Megan knew something was wrong on a daily basis but became immobile in starting to make things right. As we approach a deeper level of transparency in our lives, we must hypothetically walk inside our bodies and lifestyles to make sure we are accurately portraying ourselves in God's light. We want to be the finished hotel that was cleaned on both the inside and outside. Our bodies do more than just allow us to live on this earth. They provide the avenue by which we are to serve God in bringing Him glory. This hotel we've been given is not only a place for us to reside, but a place for others to come alongside us and stay for a day or longer. We encounter others through this hotel, or our body.

The idea our body is used to serve God and to complete His purposes for our lives require us to be transparent with ourselves and our bodies. When we are born we naturally cry for our mother's milk. Taking care of our bodies is something we must do to stay alive. We must eat food and drink enough fluids to nourish our bodies. In the beginning, we read in Genesis of God creating the earth and declaring all "good". Our view of good has been quite distorted throughout our lives. I often wonder what Adam and Eve looked like. What did "good" weight look like? They were naked and it was good. Unfortunately, sin entered the world and what was once good was destroyed.

How Adam and Eve, and the rest of humanity, looked at their own bodies was forever changed. Immediately, after taking the bite of the apple, both Adam and Eve realized they were naked and made coverings for themselves. They began to hide their bodies from one another. Their bodies became a focal point, something they now thought about, as a result of their sin. They chose to hide their bodies with clothes; in effect, they tried to cover their sin. Transparency was gone. Through centuries and countless generations we have continued the trend to hide our bodies. We struggle with how we see ourselves and the perceptions we feel others have about us.

When we struggle in any part of our lives, this affects how we interact with others and our ability to be transparent with them. Our physical being is private. I understand this is a positive thing to not see everyone and all their parts, but we need to be careful how we allow others to perceive our bodies. This desire for a positive perception of our bodies has created a huge market for clothing designers who are making millions from their designs. These clothes not only cover people but they make our bodies look much different than they really are. All the while, we pretend we look better than we really are to those around us. When we spend this much time focusing on which clothes to buy to better ourselves, we begin to place the emphasis on us. If we are honest and transparent, we begin to wear another mask through the clothing we wear. The way we perceive how others see us can become our idol.

For example, we grow up hearing how first impressions make a difference. I remember when my kids were really young and we went to the zoo. I decided to wear a pair of shorts that were also overalls. This was a functional choice for me because I had multiple pockets and three small children. I thought nothing about my choice of clothing. I was being practical in my mind! Then, there was my friend's friend, whom we'll call Alice, and whom I was meeting for the first time. The three of us, with our children, seemed to have a nice time. Again, I thought nothing more of our visit. Fast forward a few more years and my friend was going through pictures with Alice. Alice was astonished that I looked pretty. She thought I was just someone who didn't care how I looked around others.

Alice obviously struggled with how others perceived her with how she dressed. This could be a fault of mine, but I do not dress for others. I really do not care what they think, except for my husband, of course. For the most part, though, I dress for the occasion. If I go to church, I dress appropriately. However, I'm not going to get in my high heels just to look great at the grocery store. God has not called me to look stunning and ready to be on the red carpet at a moment's notice. God has called me to be beautiful in His image. This must apply in my jeans or in my red carpet attire. Let me also say, we are not called to look so pitiful that no one wants to be around us. We must be confident of who we are in God's eyes. People use clothing as a shield or a literal covering of who they are. If we feel lousy about who we are, dressing in expensive clothing might help, but will not solve the inward problem. The clothing will only medicate us for the time being.

Transparency requires us to know why we do things and what our motives might be. How you feel about your body and how you look can affect your outlook on life. The clothing you wear today might make you look great, but are you looking great because it's appropriate, or are you looking great in order to entice others? What is your motive? Are you middle-aged and trying to prove to yourself or others that you can still dress as you did in your twenties? I'm not asking you to throw off your clothing to feel good about who you are because that will only get you arrested. I'm asking you to be honest and transparent about you, how you view your body, and why you dress the way you dress.

We, as humans, can get into a physical rut and clothing can be a means to hide our out-of-shape bodies. When we are young and energetic, we get a lot of physical exercise. As we grow older, we find ourselves sitting behind a desk, or moving much less than we did when we were younger. We forget to change our physical exercise when situations change in our lives. We use time, family, or jobs as an excuse for not working out. In reality, this is the choice we have made. We have not made health a priority and must accept the responsibility for our bodies in this case. Health is our means to remain on earth.

*"As a people, we have become obsessed with Health.*
*There is something fundamentally, radically unhealthy*
*about all of this. We do not seem to be seeking more*
*exuberance in living as much as staving off failure,*

*putting off dying. We have lost all confidence in the human body."*
*– Lewis Thomas, The Medusa and the Snail, 1979*

The question we need to answer as Christians in order to be completely transparent is this, "Do we take care of our bodies well enough to fulfill God's purpose for our lives?" If we are not taking care of ourselves well enough, we are not treating our bodies as holy. We are here on this earth for a purpose. Part of that purpose involves getting the job done we are supposed to do and our bodies have to be well enough to complete the task at hand. Perhaps you do a great job taking care of your body. You eat right, you exercise, but for some reason every known ailment seems to find you and tortures your body. Your ailments might be part of your purpose. We must evaluate how well we take care of ourselves and in what areas cause us the greatest struggle to maintain a healthy body. In either case, the answer must be "yes" when asked if we can fulfill God's purpose with our bodies.

Food is a major deal in our country. We get together with friends and eat; we have church socials and eat; we celebrate birthday parties and parties at school that involve food. I don't think I need to remind you how much food is around during Thanksgiving and Christmas. Our celebrations are centered on the foods we prepare and eat. This is not really a foreign topic as we see the Passover celebration in the Bible involving Jesus and His disciples eating together. Most of the festivals in the Old Testament, if not most of them, involved eating. Eating is a natural part of our existence. Even the Israelites, in the Old Testament, had restrictions on certain foods. They knew which foods they must avoid and knew which foods they could eat. This distinction helped set them apart from pagan religions.

Remember, God created all for good. He desired for His people to be set apart from the choices of this world; thus, the restrictions on certain foods. As Christians today, we no longer follow the Old Testament law of foods of what can and cannot be eaten. So, what are we to make of this? All food is good until the idea of food becomes our focus. All food is good until it becomes gluttony. Yet, somehow, this idea of food and celebration becomes the downfall with some people when they struggle with how to separate enjoying food and enjoying time with others. They do not know how to enjoy one without the other; likewise, some cannot enjoy them both together. Food can tend to have a love/hate relationship with us and become our stumbling block.

I'll never forget the time I realized our society had it all wrong regarding food. It was my junior year in college and the girls there were worried about gaining their "college weight". I had never heard so many conversations that had to do with weight, diet, and exercise. Similarly, the summer after my junior year I decided to work at a youth camp with seventh and eighth graders. I took them to the snack shack one night and, before any of them opened up their candy, they all read the labels to see how many calories they were about to consume. They then talked about how much less they should eat the next day to compensate for what they were eating. Mind you, I appreciate the fact they were being cognizant of what they were eating, but they spent the entire snack time talking about calories instead of enjoying each other's company!

Like these girls, as we realize the importance of taking care of ourselves in order to fulfill God's plan, we must not allow "health" to become our idol and stumbling block. Instead of following the laws from the Old Testament as to what we can and cannot eat, we have chosen to follow what society tells us we should and should not eat; therefore, what we should or should not look like. We listen to all the latest health diets out there, the new pill we can take, or the latest exercise program. Health, if it becomes our idol, will cause struggles in our lives just like any other idol.

In my pursuit of being transparent, if I'm not careful, I keep health in the forefront right up there with God. All the while, I'm allowing this idea of health to literally make me sick, both physically and spiritually. Like any other area of our lives, we cannot allow "health" to control us. I remember the first time I had restrictions on what I could and couldn't eat. I was five months pregnant and the doctor told me I had to follow a certain diet. This diet was far from fun. I grumbled and complained about this new lifestyle of four months. You would have thought my life had ended. The problem was it was not my choice. I felt it was forced upon me. The simple fact is I was told certain foods were off limits and something within me made me want to rebel and eat those foods. Like Eve, I thought I might miss something since I wasn't in control.

In order to gain control, it is easy to bring our focus into the main area causing our dilemma: our health and/or our eating habits. If we become so focused in our routine of working out and eating well, though, we will miss living life in general. We become distracted in life from our true purpose of living for God. It is vital for us to keep the balance between taking care of ourselves and allowing others to be important as well. We want to make sure we have time for others versus worrying about making sure our bodies are "just right". What happens, though, when we can't gain control of what we perceive we can't have? At times we give in to things we normally would be strong against.

Paul was very transparent in Romans 7:15 when he wrote, "For what I am doing, I do not understand; for I am not practicing what I would like to do, but I am doing the very thing I hate." When we know what we shouldn't do and desire to do it anyway, it is a temptation. How does this temptation affect us spiritually? Temptation is simply a desire to do something that is wrong or unwise. Temptation itself is not a sin. It is when we give in to the temptation that we are guilty of sin. The serpent tempted Eve and she gave in to the choice of sin. She chose herself over God. What tempts one person, though, might not be an issue for another.

Once there was a professor who brought candy to class to help his students stay awake. He thought he was doing a great deed until one day a student mentioned he was struggling greatly with snacking. Each day he came to class he was faced with his temptation of food. The word "temptation" can be associated with anything, even food. During Jesus' temptation in the desert, Jesus was presented with the option to turn the stone into bread. Jesus simply replied in Matthew 4:4, "It is written, 'Man shall not live on bread alone, but on every word that proceeds out of the mouth of God.'" He chose not to use His Godly power to provide for His own needs. We must remember that God will provide for our needs and we do not need to rely upon on our strength.

Deuteronomy 28:12 states, "The LORD will open for you His good storehouse, the heavens, to give rain to your land in its season and to bless all the work of your hand; and you shall lend to many nations, but you shall not borrow." In essence, God will bless Israel so much they will have no need to ever borrow. They will be so blessed by God they will only be able to give to others. God has blessed us with an abundance of food in the United States. With this over-abundance, it becomes hard for some to know what is needed and what is simply too much. Food is not the only culprit we must deal with concerning our physical bodies.

Other areas that impact our physical bodies, like food can, are alcohol abuse, drug abuse, over-exercising, and under-exercising. These areas become an addiction for us as our focus and world seems to revolve around them in some form or fashion. I would be irresponsible if I didn't mention the impact pornography has on a person's life and view of sex. One, it degrades the person portrayed in the picture and, secondly, degrades the minds of those observing and witnessing these pictures and/or movies. Although it starts out seemingly innocent, it may lead to a sex addiction that can be their undoing. Anything that negatively affects our ability to serve God with all our heart, soul, mind, and strength is a detriment to our spiritual transparent journey.

We must continually ask ourselves what is drawing us away from God and all He desires for us. One puzzle piece at a time, we must trust God is showing us where the next piece will go. Like food, alcohol, drugs, and sex, these addictive behaviors can control us and turn us from God's purpose. We must be cognizant of what our daily habits are doing to our bodies, health, and relationships. This goes beyond what we put into our bodies and what we do with our bodies. First Corinthians 6:19-20 reads, "Or do you not know that your body is a temple of the Holy Spirit who is in you, whom you have from God, and that you are not your own? For you have been bought with a price; therefore glorify God in your body."

Scholars will talk about this passage in reference to taking care of your personal body, as well as taking care of the church body as a whole. Paul is addressing the Corinthians because their culture interacted with prostitution due to the goddess of love and sex, Aphrodite. It was said Aphrodite would bring out feelings of love and lust in others and was so beautiful that others would be enchanted by her. You might say she had a way of drawing people to her. Along with her temple, there were prostitutes who were part of the religious activity in honor of Aphrodite. When one engaged in sexual activity with a prostitute, Paul claimed they were becoming as one with the prostitute; therefore, becoming one with evil. He was trying to stress it was impossible for God and Satan to be in one person. You must choose one over the other. The bodies of those in Corinth, therefore, belonged to God and could not take part in the prostitution.

We need to decide with whom we desire to become one within our lives. Paul argued we cannot have both God and Evil at the same time. So, will we choose God or will we choose the things of this world? False religions and gods, like Aphrodite, held a big grip on the society back in Paul's time. It shaped how they reacted to other areas of their lives, including their relationship with God. Her influence was such a distraction that Paul had to address it among the Christians there in his letter to Corinth. We, likewise, have many influences on us from society to look and dress a certain way. As we desire to become transparent with ourselves, it is vital to determine whether we struggle physically in any of the areas we've talked about: body, clothing, alcohol, drugs, and sex. There is yet one other area I would like for us to discuss before we conclude the chapter.

Paul addressed those in Corinth regarding Aphrodite being a distraction. What happens when our distractions are the mere circumstances we've been dealt with in this life? What happens when our distraction is sickness? How are we to get over a distraction that is with us daily? We pray to God for healing, but don't know what we can do differently. We've done all the doctors have required of us and we feel stuck. When we talk about healing, we are begging God to make our physical bodies well. We pray for complete healing so we can live a life without the distractions of hurt, pain, and suffering. We desire more time in our calendar without all the doctors' visits and follow-ups. Just think of the time we could devote to serving God better if we didn't have this sickness and hardship in our lives. This is a very valid question.

I have struggled with this question personally with my health and that of my son. Do you know what I continually find over and over again? God shows up at the doctor's office with a person in the waiting room. My son, David, will talk to a little kid and make them smile. Or, the nurse or doctor will be so impressed with his demeanor and David will end up asking the doctor how the doctor's day is going. He is blessing others through his sicknesses. The greatest blessings have been in relating to other people. I recently spoke with a mother whose child had just been diagnosed with diabetes. She was going through everything I had been through in my own diagnosis. I also understood what it was like to watch your child dealing with an illness I could not control.

Do you know what I am? I'm a fixer. Do you know what I can't do? I can't fix myself or my son! Have you ever heard the phrase "God was just protecting me from myself?" Well, I believe if I were able to get better on my own that I would, in my humble opinion, tend to take all the credit for my health. I would look in the mirror and pat myself on the back for the job well done. You see, it would become an idol for me in a sense. If I ever consider myself over and above God, I have failed. The fact is we deal with sickness and illness due to sin in the world. I do not believe God caused us to be sick just to teach us a lesson. He can, though, teach us more about Him as we deal with these circumstances in our lives. We can choose to learn from these times or get very frustrated in the process. I lean on God more and more every day due to health.

Recently I found a CD of a sermon my dad preached years ago about healing. He doesn't usually send me his sermons, as I live out of state, but he sent this one. God used it to speak to me then and even the other day. He talked about how we ask God for healing physically. Depending on what the doctors say, we are willing to do just about anything when the prognosis is serious. But what about those times when we won't die immediately and the doctor's appointments are nothing more than an inconvenience? At those times, we can tend to push the urgency aside and continue living out our lives. The changes required by the doctor seem nothing more than a burden and too much of a change for us: mere inconveniences. If we want our bodies to become healthier, we have to be willing to listen to what the doctor says and actually do what he is asking. We can't just give him an obligatory nod, walk out of the office, and expect everything to turn out fine.

When it comes to God in our lives, we can look at it the same way. When there are small things we need to change in our lives such as eating habits, exercise habits, drug abuse issues, dressing modestly, etc., we must realize we might not die immediately from these issues. We must also realize, though, they will slowly kill us if we do not deal with them effectively. When it comes to God healing us from ourselves and from our desires, we tend to push back. It's almost as though we avoid Doctor God. We busy ourselves with busyness and distractions so we do not have to face the fact that we are sick. We react like Megan in our earlier story and ignore all the signs telling us we need to change. We say we desire to be the best Christian possible, but we do not do what we should do to get better. Let's, again, hear the struggle in Paul's voice from Romans 7:14-20:

> *"For we know that the Law is spiritual, but I am of flesh, sold into bondage to sin. For what I am doing, I do not understand; for I am not practicing what I would like to do, but I am doing the very thing I hate. But if I do the very thing I do not want to do, I agree with the Law, confessing that the Law is good. So now, no longer am I the one doing it, but sin which dwells in me. For I know that nothing good dwells in me, that is, in my flesh; for*

*the willing is present in me, but the doing of the good is not. For the good that I want, I do not do, but I practice the very evil that I do not want. But if I am doing the very thing I do not want, I am no longer the one doing it, but sin which dwells in me."*

Before Paul was the first missionary, he sought out and killed Christians. He was well educated, knew the Law, and one day encountered Christ in a very real way. He was blinded by the light of Christ until he was fully able to see as Christ saw. Even when Paul regained his earthly sight, he still struggled. We, like Paul, are blinded by what the world sees as physical expectations. We do things we know we should not do. There are the beautiful models on the runway. Looking at them through worldly eyes it would appear they have the perfect body and therefore a perfect life. What we don't see are the nights they cry because they are hungry. We don't see the days they wonder when they will stop looking beautiful. They struggle with wondering if people love them due to their looks or for the person they are on the inside. Of course, God sees them as beautiful because He created everyone in His image. Unfortunately, we tend to see ourselves as the world sees us and our idea of beautiful has become quite distorted.

*"Do you love me because I'm beautiful, or am I
beautiful because you love me?"*
*– Oscar Hammerstein*

Physical issues and expectations must honestly be assessed in our lives in order to be transparent. Some of the physical ideas we have discussed include our bodies, our health, and our addictions. How we approach these issues depend greatly on those closest to us – our family and friends. We were born into life with a preconceived notion of how life is to be lived. Our ideas are formed early with the help of our parents and those around us. As we grow older, we experience more of this world, its ideas and misconceptions of beauty and success, and our thoughts and expectations begin to form more clearly. Unfortunately, though, this culture is counter-productive to what God is calling us to do. He is calling us to be whole and complete in His beauty.

God calls us to live a godly life. This includes respecting our bodies whether we are super skinny or just big boned! We must accept ourselves just as He created us and not lean on other things or substances to make us feel fulfilled. This acceptance of ourselves includes contentment with what we have in both our bodies and our well-being. We have to accept that we will be different in this world and live our life with the contentment of our being different.

As we become transparent with our life, the question must be asked if we truly desire for God to heal us of our physical condition, our attitudes, or addictions. Are we really willing to allow Him to change us even if that means we must change our lifestyle? Whether we simply change the way we dress, choose different foods to eat, or vow to not hang around those who influence us in making poor decisions, we must realize we cannot do it on our own. We must call on God to help give us the strength we need. The deeper we get into this question of change, the more we begin to wrestle with the idea of trusting God and what He desires for our lives. Likewise, should God desire not to heal us, we must live in the contentment of His will.

He has the ultimate picture of our puzzle and not us. We must trust His will and timing in all circumstances. It's funny how that simple word "trust" can give us so many problems. As we attempt to be more real in our lives, we will find we think and act differently than those around us. For some it will be freedom in knowing they are doing God's will and living in His way. For others it will be a constant battle of realizing God's way is completely different from that of this world. They soon realize they will never look or act like those around them as they obey God's calling. Depending on how you look at the situation, you might feel a certain loss of your "previous" life. You might have to find new friends.

Your focus will no longer be on always having the best body, clothes, and lifestyle. Your focus will turn to God and what He desires for your life. No longer with the focus on us, we will see people as God sees people. Thankfully, we begin to see ourselves as God sees us. Undoubtedly, our trust will be tested as we surrender our addictions to God and His strength. We see the physical struggles our society has and the impact of these struggles upon our lives. Knowing what our physical expectations are can allow us to honestly assess whether our expectations are attainable and realistic, and whether our expectations are grounded in God or in society. We must not leave the transparency path now. It's time to be transparent with God as we work to make these changes and expectations a part of our daily routine.

## Questions:

1. How does your hotel need cleaning today? What needs to be thrown away from your life and what needs to be organized?

2. When you look in a mirror, how do you feel about your body and about how you look?

3. Who shaped your view on beauty and "looking good"? Does your view need a new perspective? How?

4. What do you do to take care of yourself physically? Are you able to fulfill what God desires for you to do in life? What areas of your life cause you to struggle with taking care of your body?

5. Do you struggle with "health" as an idol? If so, in what ways?

6. What daily habits are good and bad to your body, health, and relationships?

7. If Paul wrote a personal letter to you, what would be your distraction or Aphrodite? What steps can you take today to ease that distraction?

8. What do you do in your life that you do not want to do? What are your addictions?

## Group Transparency Exercise:

In your group, you will have those like Megan, feeling defeated by circumstances, and those like Ron, working through the circumstances. Have each participant name a distraction they face in their personal lives. Have them give an example of how it distracted them within the past week.

*Chapter 4*

# Transparency with God

*"My soul, wait in silence for God only, for my hope is
from Him. He only is my rock and my salvation, my
stronghold; I shall not be shaken. On God my salvation
and my glory rest; the rock of my strength, my refuge is
in God. Trust in Him at all times, O people; pour out
your heart before Him; God is a refuge for us."*
*– Psalm 62:5-8*

Becky just found out that her husband of forty years no longer loves
her. She had her suspicions something was not right, and she had lost
hope. She was tired of trying. She had justified in her mind, since the
kids were all grown, it didn't really matter as far as raising her family.
The reality of it was that he was already gone mentally years ago.
Would living physically alone be any different than living mentally

alone, as she had done these past five years? In her questioning, she struggled with whom to turn. Her best friend didn't have the perfect marriage, but it worked for the two of them. Her mom died last year. How Becky would have loved to pick up the phone and call her. She thought about her kids, as she was close to them, but she didn't want to get them in the middle of this. Becky felt she had nowhere to turn.

Feeling all alone, Becky warmed a nice cup of tea and sat in her favorite chair to watch some TV. Flipping from one channel to the next, she realized she was just wasting the hours until it was time to go to bed. A bit irritated with herself, and her new "life", Becky looked over at the end table and reached to get her tea. Beside her warm mug she saw the Bible she had not read since Sunday. She had nothing better to do, so she decided it wouldn't hurt to read it now. Maybe God, in His miraculous way, would decide to speak something to her, even if her faith was so small she didn't see how or why He would bother.

Her Bible opened up to the Psalms. David always seemed to be crying out to God, why couldn't she? Her eyes landed upon the scripture in Psalm 119:18-20, 24:

> *"Open my eyes, that I may behold wonderful things from Your law. I am a stranger in the earth; do not hide Your commandments from me. My soul is crushed with longing after Your ordinances at all times. Your testimonies also are my delight; they are my counselors."*

Her soul was crushed all right. It was crushed by the loss of her marriage and the loss of love from her husband. What she had not considered was if she were truly crushed with a longing after God's ordinances or laws. Were His testimonies and scriptures her delight? Were they her counselor? She began to sob as she realized the One person she had never considered to pour out her heart and struggles to was just waiting for her to enter into His presence. God longed for Becky to be transparent.

I'm sure, like Becky, we have found ourselves crushed from life, at one point or another. How we ground ourselves in the midst of these crushing events will define who we really are. Do we run to our best friend or spouse and grill them with questions? Do we call our parents and ask how we reacted when we were little? Typically we are transparent with our best friends and/or family because we can trust them with our secrets and true joys. These might be some good places to turn. But, we need to be willing and *wanting* to turn to God and to ask Him our questions. The previous examples of those we turn to in hard times are all based upon relationships and communication.

Transparency with God is simply a *relationship with open communication*. If we make God all about rules, regulations, and religion, we will sadly miss the point. These last three items, the three "R's", are man-made. They are the human attempt at understanding what our relationship should be. They can help guide us in our journey, but we cannot allow them to shackle us to where we cannot see God beyond the humanness of the rules, regulations, and religion. God is so much more than we, as mere humanity, could ever define. Many people, Christian and non-Christian alike, seem to get lost in their relationship with God because they focus on these three "R's" instead of simply loving and hanging out with God. Our open and honest relationship comes down to a simple line of communication with God.

As we deepen our relationship with God through our communication, one question we deal with, though, is, "Do we truly trust in God?" Matthew 6:25 and 30 reads: "For this reason I say to you, do not be worried about your life, as to what you will eat or what you will drink; nor for your body, as to what you will put on. Is not life more than food, and the body more than clothing? But if God so clothes the grass of the field, which is alive today and tomorrow is thrown into the furnace, will He not much more clothe you? You of little faith!" On a scale of 1-10 (with 10 being the highest) how would you rate yourself on the question of trusting God?

1    2    3    4    5    6    7    8    9    10

How did you do? Do you completely trust and do not struggle with giving God every circumstance in your life? Or, are you afraid of what God might do in and through your life if you handed everything over to Him? Are you afraid of losing "your" dreams in the face of His? In my younger days I would have circled a 9 or 10 without any hesitation. The older I get, though, I continue to find there are many more areas of my life I need to trust God with that I fear I would be below the 10. Without trust, it's hard to open up with how we are feeling. You see, I still tend to worry; therefore, I try to handle issues on my own.

Some people might not see worrying as going against trusting God. But, in reality, worry and trust cannot go hand in hand. We have been guaranteed that God will provide for our needs. So, when we worry about things to the point it overtakes our thinking and our time, we are no longer trusting God. We have made worrying into our latest "idol". We worship the "what ifs" and the "maybes" of our make believe outcomes to our present day, real situations. Our daily lives become intoxicated to what the future might hold instead of living in the reality of where we are in life.

*"When I'm trusting and being myself… Everything in my life reflects this by falling into place easily, often miraculously."*
*– Shakti Gawain*

So, have you figured out where you are in life? Do you relax fully in the knowledge you are where God wants you to be and you are making an impact for the Lord? Feeling anything except perfect on these last two questions might leave you feeling less than stellar. It is not about feeling, though, is it? Allow me to propose a concept I've learned the hard way. The times I seem to fail in the area of knowing where God wants me to be in my life and/or in my impact for God are the times I am making the situation all about me. I am becoming the "in and out" of the problem. I'm interested in the outcome because I know how it will positively or negatively affect me. I am human; therefore, I am selfish. I become my own god and try to direct the situations to the best of my interests.

Do we fully understand the concept that it's not all about us? Our lives are not the center of the universe. Let's go back to the beginning. Life for kids revolves around them. They are hungry and feel they must be fed. They are tired and want the story read now. A toy at the store catches their eyes and they pout to see if that will result in the parents buying the toy. Most of what a child experiences throughout life is wants and not needs; however, he or she perceives the circumstances as needs and not as wants. The older we become we realize most things in life are not needs, but that does not stop us from reacting as though we've been deprived when we do not get what we want. We read earlier "do not worry". If we are feeling deprived, assuming God isn't providing adequately for our needs, we become embittered and it will hinder our relationship. Therefore, this perception of needs and wants also runs over into our spiritual lives.

Webster defines a need as, "a physiological or psychological requirement for the well-being of an organism." He then defines a want in two different ways, "to be needy or destitute; to have a strong desire for." With these definitions in mind, we can assume an accurate need would be food or shelter. Can we then assume everything else is a want? If shelter is a need, though, how big of a house determines a need and how much of it is a want? Is one thousand square feet adequate or do you need five thousand? Transportation is a need to get to jobs, stores, and churches, but how much transportation do we really need versus want? Go to the internet and search for "needs versus wants" and you will find an extensive list involving university studies, PBS literature for children, and financial advice. Knowing the difference between these two areas of our lives is a true sign of maturity. By communicating with God regularly, we become aware of what is truly necessary and what our comforts are. This knowledge will help keep the things of our lives in proper perspective.

Transparency with God requires us to determine where this leaves God in the equation of needs and wants. Is He "a physiological or psychological requirement for our well-being?" Is He a want or a need in our lives? What would we do if He were not in our lives? This is purely hypothetical, of course, as God cannot be absent from our lives. He is all around and in all. He commands and it is done. He is "I AM". Fill in the blank and that is God. However, we limit God in many facets of our lives to the point we have to ask, "Do I want God so much in my life that I am truly 'desperate' for Him?" Being desperate for God means we are "in need" of Him in our lives. We realize doing things on our own is a worthless endeavor and one that will only end in failure. We must have Him to live the lives we were intended to live. This is true relationship with God.

But, what does this kind of living look like for us? It's actually an easy answer, and the simple church answer, of spending time with God, reading our Bible, and praying. This simple church answer cannot be left as a rule, regulation, or religious answer. It has to be genuine and real: a true relationship. The problem of this simple solution lies in the application of spending time with God, reading our Bible, and praying. We have to look at our lives and figure out the best way to apply God to our daily living. We must desire Him more than anything else. We must invite Him into our every day activity. We schedule a date with our spouse because of love and not because some rule says we must. Likewise, scheduling God into our lives is a good way to realize what our priority is and what it is not.

There have been times in my life I struggled with having devotions every morning at a certain time. Those struggles began in my teen years. I had so many activities and schedules to juggle, I could not seem to always fit God in every day. I told myself things would get easier with college and much easier once I started working full-time in the real world. As I was explaining my excuse to my teen leader one night, all I received was a laugh and a smile. She told me if I thought things were crazy with my schedule now, that I should just brace for the craziness of life once other people and things became a part of my schedule. As if that weren't a big enough punch in the gut, she then added that if I truly loved God, I would want to find time for Him in any circumstance in my life, and in every part of my life journey, wherever that might find me.

This began my journey of not making excuses and of holding "me" accountable for "my" decision to either include God in my life or not. This worked well enough through my teen and college years. It even sustained me while working full-time. If I didn't have time for devotions in the morning, I would eat outside in my car and quietly spend my lunch with God. It was just the two of us and I loved our relationship. Then, kids came along. This lovely interruption really complicated my ability to schedule things so neatly in my life. I truly struggled with where I was going to fit God in all of this "clutter" of extra stuff suddenly thrown at me. I didn't know how to effectively make God a part of my life. Something always threw me off!

It was during the middle of the night, when I was feeding our daughter, that I realized how alone and lost I felt. How was I to navigate raising a child in the way she should go when I couldn't even foster my own relationship with God? I felt like such a hypocrite and quite honestly a loser. Through my tears, transparency, and honest prayers to God, He lovingly reminded me that spending time with Him did not require absolute quietness. It didn't have to include my sitting with the Bible on my lap, pen and paper by my side, and a journal being written. All God wanted was me. He wanted me to fully rest in Him in whatever circumstance. So, you know what feeding times became for me? My time to sing Bible songs to my daughter! My time to rest and talk with God! It was a magical time for me to see God in a different light. We communicated differently at this point in my life, and yet He met me where I was and in my need. Thank You, God!

My communication styles and relationship with God continued to change each time that we had another child. I had to re-evaluate how I could and would spend time with God daily. There were times when I had to post Scripture on our refrigerator and read it before each meal. Breakfast and lunchtime with three small children were very trying for a stay-at-home mom with no other adult interaction! I truly needed the Lord during those days and that Scripture would get me through those meals. I felt God giving me His promise of strength and peace during that quick thirty-second read. But, it was what I needed.

There were also times when the schedule seemed to slow down, and I was given a solid thirty minutes every day to simply read, study, and write my thoughts about what God was doing in my life and those around me. This was a very real and transparent time for me to learn more about God and to seriously evaluate how I viewed God in my life during those days. I felt in those settings that God was preparing me for something. Perhaps I was being prepared for a time in the future where I wouldn't have much time to sit and digest everything I would need to get through a circumstance. You know, when those tough times came, I was able to relax and rest upon the promises He shared with me during my thirty-minute days. He stored up His truths and riches within me to get me through the drought of hardships and trials when I only had thirty seconds.

We know we have to work God into our lives to have a personal relationship with Him. But, do we really understand that our circumstances are not the same as those around us? Our relationship with God is just as personal as our relationship with our best friend or our spouse. We talk a certain language with our spouse. They get us. They know what makes us tick and when it is the appropriate time to say things. We don't know another person of the opposite sex this well, nor should we. This kind of relationship is for our spouse alone. This marriage relationship is unlike others. We are individuals who have a special bond. We, also, have certain ways of talking with our best friends. They know our history. We have inside jokes. We make time to be a part of each other's lives.

Likewise, we are all unique and have a different relationship with God. We all have different ways of talking and communicating with Him. Some enjoy writing and journaling their prayers. Others might like to recite their conversations with God in the car on the way to work. Still, some even sing songs of praise along with the radio and meet God there while driving. We are all wired differently and should not box ourselves into expecting our relationships to all be the same. Some people get lost in the three "R's" of rules, regulations, and religion at this point because they expect others to abide by the same "laws". We can allow the three "R's" to guide us in our transparency with God to some degree, but these man-made ideas cannot govern our relationships. We must all learn to live in the freedom that God has a special bond with each unique person unlike any other. Expect out of your relationship what you put into your relationship. If we spend a lot of time with God, we will learn a lot more about God. Likewise, the less time we spend with God, the more easily it will be for us to turn to other avenues during our hard times.

*"The reason why we obtain no more in prayer is
because we expect no more. God usually answers us
according to our own hearts."*
*– Richard Alleine*

We've all seen the pictures of a child kneeling beside his bed praying with his hands clasped. Some of us grew up with the kneeling position as the ideal. This position does not always work for everyone who has health conditions. Does this mean they cannot pray effective prayers? I do not think God refuses to hear our prayers because we are not on our knees. Prayer is not based on bodily position or posture, rather a matter, or posture, of the heart. But, what are we to make of this thing called prayer? Our transparency with God is all about relationship and communication. One of the best ways to deepen our communication with God is through our prayer life. We must make prayer a daily habit and a natural occurrence in our lives? Let's see how the schedules, activities, and people in our lives open the doors of communication with God through prayer.

One way to incorporate prayer in our daily lives is to pray over our calendar. Look to see what you have going on for the day and pray that God will give you the strength to face your upcoming tasks. Pray for your job and the people you will encounter. Pray your attitude in business will translate into sharing God's love to the world; whether this is through accounting, consulting, teaching, parenting, or volunteering. To be the best God has called us to be in our activities, integrity, and attitudes, we have to have the Holy Spirit living in us. We need to be empowered by His very presence within our lives.

Secondly, we can pray for the activities, or calendars, of those around us. When did you last pray for your spouse? He or she not only needs your emotional support, but your spiritual support. We should pray for God's blessings upon our spouse and the work he or she does on a daily basis. Pray that others will be impacted by his example. Pray he will be the father he needs to be or she will be the mother she needs to be. We are all flawed. We know our spouse pretty well. Pray for those flaws. Pray that the devil will not have a foothold in that area of his or her life. Once we start praying for our spouse, our eyes will open to how we can better support him or her in these areas.

Similarly, if God has entrusted children to you, you must incorporate prayer for your children into your routine. Pray for them as they go to school in the morning. Pray for them at lunchtime to continue to make right choices at school. They have many people influencing their lives. Pray not only for those children they come in contact with daily, but for their teachers. Pray their teachers will know how to effectively teach your child and your child's class. Lots of patience is needed in a classroom of twenty or more kids. Patience, kindness, and love can never be prayed about enough. Send up your prayers.

Another way to pray for your children is to pray for their future spouses. Having a hard time raising your kids and feeling like you are setting them up for a lot of counseling in the future? Pray for your kids' future in-laws. They might be having a hard time raising your future sons or daughters-in-law. Those future sons or daughters-in-law will strongly affect your children one day as they begin their own family.

Prayer cannot begin soon enough. As you begin praying over your calendar, spouse, and children, God will communicate to you in areas where you can help teach, lead, or walk alongside your loved ones in support. God desires to do the same for us. He longs for us to desire His leading. He can nudge us while we pray. As He nudges us, we learn His desires and a bit more about His character. We begin to grow in a deeper relationship with God.

Last, by not least, an empowering way to pray is praying Scripture. This can be a Scripture verse you recently read, or a verse you have on your refrigerator to see multiple times each day. It can be a pertinent verse for your life at a certain time. In whatever area of my life I'm struggling with at any certain point in my life, I find a Scripture that will empower me to choose God and not my own path. Can you imagine saying the words of God back to God? These are His words. If you say Scriptures with truth and conviction, your heart will be moved. "According to a word of Scripture we pray for the clarification of our day, for preservation from sin, for growth in sanctification, for faithfulness and strength in our work. And we may be certain that our prayer will be heard, because it is a response to God's Word and promise. Because God's Word has found its fulfillment in Jesus Christ, all prayers that we pray conforming to this Word are certainly heard and answered in Jesus Christ" (Bonhoeffer 1954, 85).

Recently, I have enjoyed parts of Psalm 119 in my Scripture praying. A few weeks ago I heard some really disturbing news about a friend of mine and a bad choice that was made. This choice not only ended a career, but it was far-reaching to hundreds. I was crushed. I really knew this person and didn't know how something like this could have happened. Why was there a compromise? I was so confused. Nothing seemed to make any sense. So, I cried out to God. In most circumstances I have asked the "why" questions. Over and over again, though, my questions resonated with the "I just don't understand."

I opened my Bible and began reading. I found my way to Psalm 119:26-27 and read the following: "I have told of my ways, and You have answered me; teach me Your statues. Make me understand the way of Your precepts, so I will meditate on Your wonders." I further read in verses 33-38, "Teach me, O LORD, the way of Your statues, and I shall observe it to the end. Give me understanding, that I may observe Your law and keep it with all my heart. Make me walk in the path of Your commandments, for I delight in it. Incline my heart to Your testimonies and not to dishonest gain. Turn away my eyes from looking at vanity, and revive me in Your ways. Establish Your word to Your servant, as that which produces reverence for You."

Perhaps I was being a bit demanding of God...teach me, make me, teach me, give me, make me, establish. I would like to think if the psalmist prayed this prayer, than I could, as well, and I did. Not only did I read it once, I then prayed it and cried out to God one more time. I was really confused and confounded in this situation. PLEASE, GOD, MAKE ME UNDERSTAND!!! Unfortunately, this situation was not the first time I have come to question what was going on around me. After having such a great relationship with God, I wondered how this godly friend could fall so quickly. Know what really scared me as I screamed out, "Make me understand"? How far away am I from falling so quickly and choosing what this world has to offer? What would it take in my life for me to turn my face from God? Would my falling impact just my family or hundreds? The impact of sin affects generations upon generations. Thankfully, the reverse is also true, our choosing God impacts generations upon generations more than the impact of sin.

I looked again at Scripture and found verses 28-31, "My soul weeps because of grief; strengthen me according to Your word. Remove the false way from me, and graciously grant me Your law. I have chosen the faithful way; I have placed Your ordinances before me. I cling to Your testimonies; O LORD, do not put me to shame! I shall run the way of Your commandments, for You will enlarge my heart." Yes, I was grieved, but my strength came not out of false hope from this earth, but from God's word. I begged God to take any false ways from me. I prayed He would instill His word in my heart. I vowed again to choose His ways.

I realized, at this point in time, I based my life upon His words and asked Him to come through for me. My religion that had helped form and shape me had grown fully into a relationship where I could approach the throne of grace confidently. I needed to know He was legit. I approached Him with my questions. My determination to believe God was truly "just and good" allowed me to continue leading this life of love because it was only through God's grace and strength that I found freedom in His law. The law was no longer a list of rules or regulations, but a point of respect and love. I continued to pray for Him to make me understand this circumstance as I desired to know Him more fully.

The beautiful thing I love about Psalm 119 is the relationship between the psalmist and God. The writer of this psalm pours out his heart to God because he saw the evil around him in this world. As I mentioned earlier, it came across a bit demanding of God as the psalmist prayed "teach me, make me, teach me, give me, make me, establish". I had to look at the rest of the psalm to understand their relationship. You see, this writer showed his devotion to God by stating, "I have chosen, I have placed, I cling, I shall run." He was devoted to God by his actions and lifestyle; likewise, God answered. "The purpose of God's positive direction and protection from evil is to encourage the psalmist to keep the law. Keeping the law was not a matter of external conformity in the Old Testament but required "a Heart" of absolute devotion to God" (Gaebelein 1991, 5:744).

We learn through this psalm, as in many others, that the relationship is not based on law or rules and regulations alone; it is about heart and a relationship. It is not a one-sided conversation, either. God created man for relationship with Him because He desires us. Seeing that God made us and desires us, I believe this means He already has the heart for this relationship; therefore, the motivation has to come from our end. We have to work on our heart, and how the issues of our lives affect our relationship with God. Through the power of prayer in our lives, we have access to an open communication with God.

One weakness of those growing up in the church that must be overcome is the God-blaming card. In order to keep transparency real with God and not blame Him for our actions, we must acknowledge the fact that when we make bad choices there are obvious consequences to our decisions. We have to acknowledge the reality of what happens because of our behavior and not play the guilt and shame game with God. When we do something wrong and feel guilty for what we've done, we feel conviction for the sin we've committed. If we do not respond to God and ask for forgiveness, it's easy to then blame God for allowing bad things to happen to us. In reality, most of the time, these bad things are consequences of our actions. We blame God because we do not want to blame ourselves or admit, and be transparent, to ourselves about what we have done. As we play the blame game, we are not being transparent with both ourselves and God.

This dishonesty between God and us causes separation in our relationship. This separation is from our side of the story since God is fully present in our lives and never desires for us to be apart. Sadly, the longer we are dishonest and realize there is something wrong in our relationship, the less we are inclined to approach God with our questions. More often than not, we really don't know where to begin. We are ashamed to even ask God for help and become angry that all is not right in our life and in our relationship. This anger and dissatisfaction overshadows everything. We lose our focus on God and try to figure out how to better our lives and the situation on our own.

So, how are we to draw back to God and be transparent? A choice has to be made. There has to be a choice to desire God in our lives. There needs to be repentance of the sin we have committed. This sin might be as simple as lying to your parents or as complicated as adultery. It could be the sin of apathy. Sin is sin, in all reality, and is a separation from God. We must ask for forgiveness of trying to live life on our own strength whether we are a new Christian or have been a Christian for many years. If we are truly transparent about what sin does for our relationship with God, we must admit and see that sin is a rejection of God's love. Simply put, God is good no matter the circumstance. He desires all to live in a right relationship with Him.

What are we to make of the times when bad things happen to good people? On these occasions, life stinks and we need to remember not everything is a personal spiritual issue. Sickness, disease, hurt, and hard labor was not God's original plan for man, but came into the world due to Adam's sin; therefore, none of us are immune to these trials of life. Some of these problems we encounter throughout life are simply a result of a fallen humanity; whether through sin of others or sin of our own. Through prayer and meditation on God's Word, we are able to discern whether our circumstances are simply life happening around us or a spiritual issue needing to be addressed.

Recently my friend's sister-in-law went into labor with their fifth child. Complications ensued and she never came home from the hospital. During this two-week time frame, her husband was giving updates on Facebook. Their story had been shared over and over again.

People from all over the world were sending in their comments and prayers. It seemed like such a sad situation; yet, there were many miracles in this situation. God healed her in a real and complete way; He healed her from her earthly body. Their beautiful baby girl is at home and alive. So many people were brought together during this time of prayer and community. Her story touched me even though I never met this godly woman. I knew her husband from college only through his brother and sister-in-law. But their story resonates with any and all of us. During our most difficult circumstances, when life stinks, will we choose to praise the Lord as he did? Will we choose to continue to believe in God when things of this earth are taken away or do we love things of this earth more than God?

When times are difficult, and life stinks, we struggle to be transparent with God because of the many unanswered questions. Transparency is easier for most while everything is going well. I never had a hard time looking into my parents' eyes when I had listened and obeyed them. But, the times when I had questions, or felt hurt over a situation, those were the times I struggled to understand. I would go to them with questions, and I would express how my side of the story felt. Most times I would leave those conversations satisfied, but not always. There were a few times I decided I would simply choose to trust them in their decisions, which was not at all easy for me. This same situation applies to our relationship with God where the questions must be asked in the difficult times. Our questioning though, does not guarantee the answers we might desire.

What do we do when the difficult times come, and it's hard to be transparent with God? The times bad things happen to us and we feel we did nothing to deserve our circumstances? Do we talk to God or do we sulk and determine He must be against us somehow? What about the difficult questions of life? Why allow a mother of five young girls to die? Why does cancer happen to both old and young alike? How can these situations be used for good? I find these difficult times easier to endure when I walk into God's presence and read His words and Scripture. I draw near to God in our relationship and somehow miraculously feel Him drawing near to me. Do not get me wrong, I still approach God with many questions; however, I still choose to approach Him and communicate with Him.

Christians, and non-Christians alike, are not immune to the evil in this world because humanity was given a choice. Again, God desires transparency in our relationship with Him so much that he gave us a choice of whether we love and choose Him or reject His love and choose ourselves. While this choice seems to offer much freedom to the Christian, it can also cause us to fret at times when we feel God is not calling us to do what we desire to do with our lives. We will either choose God's path or our own path. During this decision-making time, we must be transparent enough with God to ask Him what He desires of our lives. If His purpose is not our choosing, we must approach the throne of grace with confidence knowing He can handle our questioning. I truly believe God would rather have us approaching His throne with questioning than to turn our back on Him.

As we commune with God on a more consistent basis, our questioning of God and what is going on around us will not seem like questioning but rather a simple conversation between friends. We will slowly begin to see things from His perspective. Just as we begin to mimic and act like others we hang out with regularly, we will begin to mimic God. Through prayer, we grow deeper with God and can see Him moving in our lives. Once we are in tune with God, our desire to pray for others and their situations will increase. Our desire to grow deeper will multiply and our love for God's Word will come alive. We will begin to thank God for what He is doing around us and will not be able to stop praising Him for Who He is. Our praise and adoration for God is a great outpouring of our love of God. Through this time of praising God, we will realize, like a self-fulfilling prophecy, how much more we love Him and why we love Him.

Being transparent with God is as simple as loving Him for who He is, loving ourselves for who He made us to be, and keeping the lines of communication open continually. It is a place where we let go of the three "R's" of religion, rules, and regulations, and learn to trust. Transparency with God is nothing more than communication and relationship. It is a place for us to commune with God, open our hearts to Him, and open our eyes to see how He sees. This transparency reveals to us that God truly is good at all times no matter the circumstances in our lives. It is an adventure well worth our time and attention.

## *Questions*

1. How do you explain worrying and trusting in God? How do they compare and how are they different?

2. What things do you worry about most on a daily basis?

3. Do you compare your relationship with God to others' relationship with God? How does that hinder or help you?

4. What inhibits you from a daily walk with God? Schedules, life choices, or a lack of desire?

5. What are some steps you can do today to help you in your walk with God?

6. Do you find it easy to pray? Why or why not? What makes praying hard for you?

7.  Is it easier to pray for yourself or others? Why is this?

8.  How do we react to God when difficult circumstances come our way?

9.  How do you explain our loving God to those in this world when bad things happen?

10. Where are you in your transparency with God?

### Group Transparency Exercise.

Have each member of your group name a specific time in their lives when they struggled to see God as good. Who and/or what allowed or prevented them from overcoming this perception of God not being good?

*Chapter 5*

# Transparency with Others

We are well on our way to understanding transparency in our personal lives and with God. We have learned transparency must be a part of our lives. It is vital for us to know our story, to be open about our expectations of life, to be honest with ourselves about our physical beings, and to communicate with God in our relationship with Him. By seeing ourselves as God sees us, we will be able to grow deeper with God. How do we translate our openness with God to others? Do others really matter in our pursuit of being transparent? If so, how can we let them into our lives without losing ourselves, our sanity, and our privacy? What about when others have it all together? How are we to relate to them when we feel we don't have it all together? These are the times we must turn to God to know how much to open up with others and to whom we share our lives.

It is important for us to feel as though we belong to someone else besides ourselves. With that being said, most of us have been hurt one time or another and this makes it very difficult for us to move forward in trusting and being transparent with others. We honestly feel we can make it through most things on our own and our self-reliance goes against being transparent. This idea of transparency makes us appear weak and in need of help. Our self-disclosure will only cause the pain to surface again in our lives and quite possibly make us look overly emotional. With all these possibilities in mind, we wonder why we would risk embarrassment or more heartache in the name of being transparent.

We continually compare ourselves with others and this affects our lifestyles and our relationship with materialism. This comparison can be what challenges us to excellence, or it can be our downfall. Some people grow up with next to nothing, work hard, and are very successful. Seeing what others have in this life has motivated them in a positive manner. Others grow up with a lot of money, work hard, and are baffled when they can't seem to afford the things others have. In a country where wealth is so abundant, and our options of things to buy seem limitless, we easily become numb to our pursuit of "extra things" in our lives. If we are not careful, this pursuit can distract us from our transparency journey. We must become aware of the grip materialism has on our culture and how it impacts our lives with or without our consent.

In order to gain the proper perspective in being transparent with others, we need to start with the Bible. Paul addresses our helping each other in 2 Corinthians 1:3-5, "Blessed be the God and Father of our Lord Jesus Christ, the Father of mercies and God of all comfort, who comforts us in all our affliction so that we will be able to comfort those who are in any affliction with the comfort with which we ourselves are comforted by God. For just as the sufferings of Christ are ours in abundance, so also our comfort is abundant through Christ." God calls us to bear one another's burdens and to comfort those around us. We cannot do this unless we are aware of their afflictions and they cannot comfort us without knowing our afflictions; therefore, we must glean from this passage of Scripture that transparency with others is a Biblical viewpoint. With that being said, how do we begin to plunge forward in our transparency with others when we are legitimately afraid of the outcome?

Let's start with the most ideal situation. You have grown up in your community and have a tight group of friends. The five of you have been through everything together. You know each others' struggles, weaknesses, bad decisions, and good decisions. You have been together through your marriages, the birth of your kids, and now your kids leaving home. All of you attend church regularly and have a great relationship with God. You hold each other accountable spiritually every week during your Bible Study. Nothing is off-limits when asking for prayer requests or for help in general. This support group is your backbone and life through your Christian walk.

You have never worried about this group "leaking" information to others outside your group because you have vowed confidentiality. Even throughout the week, you have those in the group asking about your week and how they can pray for you in a better, more specific way. This group desires your spiritual growth as much as they desire their own personal growth. You all understand that as one of you grows, the others will grow. You are pulling each other along the journey of life in a real and positive way. Your children talk to the others in the group as though they are second parents to them. This is your ideal situation and one that God looks down upon and smiles.

Now, let's look at a not-so-ideal situation. You sign up for a small group at your church. There are some people you know really well and others you've never met. After some time, you believe those in the group are ready to open up and you begin to share deeply from your heart. You share an area of your life where you are truly struggling; knowing someone in your job position and "spiritual stature" should not be struggling with this. As you share, a young Christian in the group is taken aback and looks at you in horror. It, unfortunately, does not end there. This person tells someone outside of your group and your struggle is now common knowledge. You start to shut down, become more introspective, and begin to guard against what words will be spoken in the future. You, like Adam and Eve, "clothe" yourself with fig leaves in shame. Where did it all go wrong?

*The first reason we struggle in our transparency with others is because of selfish desires and tendencies.* Selfishness can be a bad and very destructive emotion. Just like Eve wanted to be like God and ate the fruit, we, too, desire to be like God. We want to be the best at everything and will do most anything to appear to be above someone else. This can include putting them down and sharing their weaknesses with others in order to make ourselves look better. A professor once taught on the commandment of "do not kill". I always heard "do not kill" as "do not murder and end someone's life". But, during this lesson, he equated gossiping and sharing weaknesses unnecessarily to the murdering of a person's character. I thought it was a bit far-fetched; nevertheless, I couldn't stop thinking about it for weeks.

I began to see how murdering another person's character might be far worse for that person than if they had physically been killed. They must live daily with what others think and know about them. For those of you who enjoy reading, you will remember the book *To Kill A Mockingbird* by Harper Lee. In this book, Tom, a black man, is wrongly accused of a crime because the completely white and prejudiced jury believed he was guilty based on his skin color. After the trial, Tom decides he cannot live with people thinking he did something wrong. He escapes from jail and is killed in the process. The slaughtering of his character not only killed him emotionally, but ultimately physically. He could not live with the injustice of what was done to him, and it was unbearable for him.

If we are not careful, we, too, can murder someone's character by saying things unnecessarily. Sharing prayer requests can be a form of gossiping if it's not done with the proper intent. Sometimes people enjoy the prayer request time because they see it as getting to know peoples' business that they can save for a later time to "speak the truth" at their discretion. For example, Nicole had a rough time in high school and made some bad decisions which led to years of therapy during college. As she was sharing this time of her life with her college group, she was being real and truthful about what she did and how sorry she was for her mistakes. Now that she is fifty, it no longer is a prayer request. If any person in the college group shared the information with someone at this point, it would be the truth, but it might taint, or murder, Nicole's character.

*The second reason we struggle in our transparency with others is due to embarrassment or vulnerability.* If we are made a fool in front of everyone, or worse, wrongly accused of doing something, like Tom, we live with that consequence every day. We are then faced with two choices: we can choose to allow this hardship to shape our lives or we can choose to move on with our lives. Steven Kalas wrote the following in his article, "It's Easy to Ruin a Person's Reputation":

> *"So, how do ruined people pick up and move on*
> *again toward a thriving, grateful life? I think the first*
> *order of business is surrender. We stop railing against*

*the injustice. Somewhere inside of ourselves, we make an authentic peace with the fact that no one is immune to injustice. We decide to deeply believe that we waste our lives insisting every scale must be balanced before we are free.*

*Second, in some cases, we walk away from the fight. Yes, we give up. We acknowledge that our enemy has won and move on to other work, other opportunities to give life a chance.*

*And lastly, we decide that no one has the power to make life anything less than good. I guess you might call this decision a decision of faith, even if you aren't religious" (Kalas February 28, 2012).*

This is not a religious article and yet it completely applies to us in our transparency journey. "Surrender" is a must for all of us as we become vulnerable with others. Through our transparency, we realize we are part of a "messed-up" life that is neither fair nor right in everyone's eyes. Good things will happen to both good and bad people; likewise, bad will happen to all. It is up to us to see others through the eyes of God, and we must give them the benefit of the doubt as they are on this journey of life. As we surrender our lives to God through our trials, we realize others around us are hurting, as well. We are not alone in our sufferings and parts of our lives will be lost if we continue to live in this hurt.

Not wanting to live in this hurt leads us to the second point Kalas mentioned: "giving up". We allow the other person to win and must decide what others do with the knowledge of our lives depend upon them and not us. We must give up control over our situation when it becomes known to others. We need to walk away with our head held high although we are completely confused and dumbfounded as to why anyone would wrongly accuse us or maliciously spread what is embarrassing to us. It is easy to feel betrayed and quite belittled; yet, fighting back will get us nowhere. This vulnerability with others might be embarrassing, but that part of our past is who we were at some point and it has shaped us. It does not have to define us though, no matter who is aware of our circumstances. We will be enslaved to others if we run away from who we are, so we leave it alone and let the accusations die. This takes a lot of maturity in our lives.

If we are finding our sense of purpose in God alone, and not in others' expectations or thoughts about us, this will be a bit easier. We will not be as concerned with what others think; we will be concerned with God and His glory. This goes along with the last point Kalas mentioned of our deciding "life goes on after all". The question still remains, though, how are we to get to that point of being transparent with others? We just do it! Within the proper boundaries, and using our commonsense, we will have to ask God what level of sharing is appropriate. Again, recall that we cannot be appropriately and truly transparent, like Adam and Eve, unless we are in a right relationship with God.

Often we are so burdened and overwhelmed with other thoughts, images, and concerns that it may take a long time before God's Word has swept all else aside and come through (Bonhoeffer 1954, 82). Again, we think of ourselves quite a bit and are inherently selfish. This will impede our relationships with others in a significant manner. Let's look back at the group who did not do well with their confidentiality. The person who betrayed confidentiality was selfish and wanted to better himself. The "little secret" that was shared made him feel more important and was an embarrassment to the person who was truly vulnerable and shared with the group. Having others know the "bad things" about us, or simply our mistakes, makes us feel we look bad, weak, and vulnerable in their eyes.

*This brings us to the third struggle with transparency: our vulnerability with others proves we are not perfect.* Can you tell me the name of one person, besides Jesus, who lived a completely perfect life? I can't. Why do we consistently think others expect our lives to be perfect? If we are so quick to offer grace to others, knowing they make mistakes, why can't we grant ourselves the same grace? If we were to do this, we would be more apt to share those times when we mess up in both small and big areas of our lives. This sharing will, in effect, encourage others throughout their lives as they try to maneuver through their ups and downs. God has called us to share others' burdens; as a Christian, it is our act of worship to help those around us to draw closer to God through our circumstances and not for us to pretend that everything in our lives is perfect. If we pretend to have it all together, we basically are pretending and living a lie. Doesn't sound much like a Christian, does it?

For those struggling to let go of the "perfect" life, being open with others about our struggles reveals our weaknesses and hurts our pride. *Pride is the fourth reason we have a hard time with transparency and admitting to others we are struggling.* This takes a lot of courage. It's much easier for us to bear others' burdens and listen to their problems than to admit we struggle, as well, and have our own issues. We should not forget what the Bible says in Matthew 7:4–5, "Or how can you say to your brother, 'Let me take the speck out of your eye,' and behold, the log is in your own eye? You hypocrite, first take the log out of your own eye, and then you will see clearly to take the speck out of your brother's eye."

While we work through what we need to change in our lives, it might be easier to focus upon someone else's life and how we could fix them. If we were to put that same energy and focus upon our own lives, we would be able to solve many of our own problems and have less "specks" or "logs" in our own eyes. The problem comes with the actual removing of the logs. Most of these removals will cause us to make changes in our lives...some more painful than others. If it were truly easy to get rid of them, we would not struggle. Unfortunately, though, they typically require a different way of thinking or a change in how we are currently living. They require us to remove them by opening up with others instead of expecting others to open up.

We must be willing to trust others with our burdens, just as we expect others to trust us with their burdens. *This fifth reason of struggling with transparency, as we discussed previously, requires for us to have a good understanding of where we are in life through God's eyes.* Most people will find they constantly struggle with trust if they cannot trust themselves or trust God. I found this to be true in my life during a dark period of my life. What I didn't expect was for God to send someone, who later became my wonderful husband, to show me I could trust another person with every part of my life. I fell in love more with God as I fell more in love with my husband. I figured if I was able to trust a human being as much as him, how much more could I expect to trust God? If my husband desired good in my life, how much more did God desire good for me? This transparency with my husband furthered my relationship with God and brought me to a deeper understanding of Him.

I have seen relationships grow due to accountability and transparency many times over and I have seen others hurt by this transparency. *It is true that you will lose some of your privacy with transparency and is the sixth reason people struggle to share with others.* They want to be their own person and have control over their own lives. They never know if they will turn around and others will know what they have shared with others. Remember, our sharing must be in accordance with what God desires for you to share with others. God did not create the majority of us to expose all of our sins and/or heartaches with the entire world. We have people who were created specifically to carry our burdens, and we have people with whom we are to share their burdens. We might be accountable with the same people for our entire lives and still have others coming and going in and out of our lives. Some of the people who have had the most impact upon my life are those I've only known briefly. Yet, the ones I've known for a long time have provided the day-to-day stability I needed even though my privacy was gone.

*In our transparency with others, losing our privacy and admitting our weaknesses to others causes us to struggle in a seventh area: self-reliance.* We are taught when we are younger to do things on our own and not rely upon others. As this develops in our minds the older we become, we struggle to open up to others simply because it proves to us that we cannot do everything on our own. This deals with pride in some ways. In other ways, we try to fill the void, and the realization that we can't do everything on our own by surrounding ourselves with things gives a false hope of self-reliance. Placing importance on things in and around our lives can be quite destructive.

*The eighth area of our lives that makes it harder to be open in our transparency with others is materialism.* Most people, in fact, are unaware of how much this obsession with material goods and material gain affects them. Webster defines materialism as, "a doctrine that the only or the highest values or objectives lie in material well-being and in the furtherance of material progress; and, a preoccupation with or stress upon material rather than intellectual or spiritual things." Essentially, we place importance on things and not relationships. Remember when we discussed how anything that gets our attention more than God has become our idol? The same thing applies here. We can never allow things to get in our way and/or relationship with God and others.

We have a great need to feel fulfilled physically and materialism is something used to soften this desire. It is used to fill a hole that can never be truly filled without God. You build a house and buy nice furnishings so others think you have it together when they come over. Not only are there nice things in your house, but you drape yourself in the finest clothing. Your cars are shiny and your electronics are top-notch. It seems it's all you could ever want, but it's never enough to fill the emptiness. The desire for more things and the best things is simply a mask we use to fill this hole, and can become a downfall for people as it replaces the relationships God intended for our lives.

What happens when we allow things to get in our way? This concept of things and their importance impacts how we see others and how we relate to them. Some people might be struggling to find themselves and their self-worth through possessions and lose those relationships around them in the process. Whether or not materialism is a known addiction in their lives, these people can be cruel and callous in their attempt to get what they want. They will work long hours, avoiding their families and friends in the process, just to feed their passion for more stuff. This lifestyle is not conducive in being transparent with others since a desire for relationship with others is second to that of objects.

One problem we have with materialism and transparency is that we tend to base whether someone has it all together by what they materially have in life. We look to see how successful they are by the house they own, or whether they seem genuinely happy in life, in marriage and relationships, or in their job. We look at our neighbors and they appear to have it all together as they take many trips, have the latest clothing styles, and have their children active in sports. Our focus becomes centered on what they have on the outside and not what is on the inside. Stuff literally clutters our view of others and we struggle to see the heart of people like God sees them.

The second problem we have with materialism and transparency is we are constantly comparing our lives with that of others. We compare ourselves to others whether we consciously think about it this way and struggle to keep up with the Jones's in our lives. This proves to be a distraction more than anything as it's a constant pursuit of other things, whether physical or emotional. The more people realize they don't have what the Jones's have, the more they adjust their goals to better attain what others have without being aware of the impact of materialism on their lives. It becomes as simple as seeing something they desire, like Aphrodite in Corinth, and are enticed until they get what they want. If we are not careful and focused on God's desires for our lives, we will begin to compete with what others have and leave God in the background.

*"Beauty in things exists in the mind which*
*contemplates them."*
*– David Hume*

This comparison with others affects our transparency with them because we feel we cannot relate with them if they appear to have more than we have. Likewise, we will not feel we can relate if they appear to have everything together. I remember going on a mission trip the year after I graduated from college and we were told to bring old clothes as they would get dirty and it was a poor country. I remember going out and buying clothes I didn't mind getting dirty and that appeared old and not dressy. The guilt I felt when I saw others in that country struggling to live was huge and here I was just joking the week prior about having to buy "old" clothes. My guilt with having more materially than those in that country almost became an obstacle for me to open up to them and be transparent about what we had in common: God! The things of this life got in my way on that journey.

This desire for materialism also causes us to live beneath our God-given talents and abilities in order to obtain what others have. God did not call us to live below our talents. He called us to live for Him and to live out His plan and purpose for our lives. This means we are to put our jobs in the proper perspective, be willing to give up what our society considers great, and use our talents and abilities to further His kingdom. The father or mother who is never at home because he or she is busy working for the next promotion, car, or toy has forgotten his or her calling to raise the next generation to be God's disciples in this fallen world. God called us to use our talents wisely. The influence that material goods has on our society is great, and it is up to us to decide if we will allow that to control how we live our lives or if we will control how much it influences what we buy and obtain.

We have discussed several issues that hinder our transparency with others: selfishness, embarrassment, vulnerability, perfection, weakness, pride, trust, privacy, self-reliance, materialism, and comparison to others. With so many issues to overcome, we all might be ready to throw in the towel and call it quits. There are many examples we could give in our personal lives that would reiterate why being transparent with others is a dangerous thing. But, since we have talked about transparency with others while looking at the glass half-empty, it's only fair we approach it while seeing the glass half-full.

As a child, most Sunday meals consisted of roast, potatoes, and carrots cooked together for better flavoring. The longer it cooked the better it tasted! No one had to ask what was on the lunch menu that day as the roast, potatoes, and carrots were a Sunday constant at our house. We don't always have roast on Sundays, now that I'm grown, but I love how easy it can all come together. One day as I was preparing the food though, I found my potatoes were rotten and I could only cook the carrots with the roast. I found some green beans to serve with the meal, but it just wasn't the same. Another time I ventured out and didn't do either carrots or potatoes. Talk about an unpleasant experience because the meal wasn't how it was supposed to be! I desperately missed my carrots and potatoes and how the flavor of the roast would seep into the carrots and potatoes to make them soft and flavorful. I wondered why I would even try to venture from this meal in the future and mess up perfection. Each part alone was edible and good; together, though, they were great.

In our lives, God is the roast, we are the carrots, and others are the potatoes. God could do this thing called life on His own, but it's so much better with all of us together. The longer we marinate and rest with God, the more of His flavoring we will absorb and the more He will make us soft and flavorful. Our hearts will not be hardened by things of this world to the point we are untouchable and unreachable. Rather, we will be soft and pliable to see as God sees and to be used as He desires. Yet, we try to venture from this meal God has designed for us and this is where we experience our unpleasant experiences. We were meant to go hand-in-hand with God and others in our transparency journey.

This transparency is vital for our spiritual journey. Whatever God gave us for our journey is not meant for us alone, but meant to be shared with others so we might grow together in His care. As Christians, it is vital for us to be honest with ourselves on the impact others have on our lives, whether positively or negatively. We must address the times we have been hurt by others and, with God's help, forgive them. We must also ask others to forgive us when we have wronged them. These tendencies to forgive and be forgiven are not natural to many of us as we struggle with our pride and self-reliance. This forgiveness means we desire to show God's love to those who might not deserve our forgiveness; yet, Jesus did this very thing for us.

Let's think again about the ideal small group with which you can share and be transparent. It is a group where each participant is actively growing in a relationship with God. Should a person fail and "leak" confidential information, they would be convicted of what they have done by the Holy Spirit and would seek forgiveness from both God and the person they wronged. It is a group where you realize people, by their very nature, are not perfect. Mistakes will be made and we will be hurt by others. By asking God whom we can trust and how much we should share with a group or certain individuals, our relationships of accountability will grow. This growth will give us hope that transparency has a proper place in our journey.

What types of sharing you do with others will depend on your circumstances and personal situations. Asking for prayer over a circumstance is not a sign of weakness; rather, it is a sign of great faith. You are admitting to leaving your problems in God's hands and addressing the fact that it is hard to leave it there. This is the very reason you ask for prayer. This sharing of life allows for a greater sense of accountability. Studies have been done on people who diet alone versus with a partner. Those who choose to go at it alone are at a greater risk of failure than those who choose to have accountability. The same thing goes for giving up addictions, bad habits, and starting new habits; therefore, we can apply this accountability to our spiritual lives if we desire greater change.

Since many of us have had a bad experience with being transparent with others, let's look at the example Jesus set for us. He was transparent with His family as He chose to stay behind in Jerusalem to teach in the temple instead of journeying home. He knew His story and His story was about spreading God's Word. At the start of His ministry, he walked up to John the Baptist and they had a moment of true transparency. John felt unworthy to baptize Jesus and Jesus responds by confirming John's ministry. As John baptized Him, Jesus came out of the water and God spoke from heaven declaring that Jesus was His Son. Jesus then journeyed into the desert to be tempted for forty days and nights. He was tempted on our common issues of providing for ourselves, pride, and making ourselves a god. Jesus, in His sinless life, was transparent with the devil as He used Scripture to combat him and chose God over Himself and the devil all three times. Jesus then left the desert and His time of temptations, and made His way back to Galilee where He chose His twelve disciples. In His transparency with others, He spoke His mind and what He knew to be true.

Over the next three years, Jesus ministered to the crowds and taught the people and His disciples about God's kingdom. He healed people He had never met before and even empowered His disciples to heal others. He explained parables to them and even shared what the future would hold, even when they didn't seem to understand. Jesus was sharing Himself and being transparent with what was to come. Throughout this time of teaching and ministry though, Jesus would withdraw Himself from the crowd for some alone time to pray and communicate with God. In the gospels of Matthew and Mark we read of one such night when Jesus sent His disciples ahead of Him in the boat and withdrew Himself from the crowd. Later, as He joined them, they would be scared He was a ghost.

Jesus had been communicating with God right before He encountered the lack of faith from His closest friends. Through this bond with God, He was able to function properly while communicating with them because He was already focused upon what God wanted in His life. As we already know, we have to be transparent with God and ourselves. I don't think it's possible to be truly transparent and open with others if we don't have our relationship with God on the right track. If we do not understand who we are, then how can we interact with others? How do we have a true opinion about anything, for that matter, if we do not sincerely know how we feel? It is a continual self-evaluation of who we are in God. This last part is vital...we must constantly remain in God.

Jesus knew this to be true and is why He would withdraw Himself from the crowds and those closest to Him. Luke 5:16 reads, "But Jesus Himself would often slip away to the wilderness and pray." He took time to interact with God and approach Him. Even at the end of His ministry we read in Luke 22:39-42, "And He came out and proceeded as was His custom to the Mount of Olives; and the disciples also followed Him. When He arrived at the place, He said to them, 'Pray that you may not enter into temptation.' And He withdrew from them about a stone's throw, and He knelt down and began to pray, saying, 'Father, if You are willing, remove this cup from Me; yet not My will, but Yours be done.'" Retreating to pray was Jesus' custom. He discovered God's will during these times.

Jesus did a great job of keeping things in perspective and in the right order. He knew who He was supposed to be and what He was supposed to do according to God's desires, and He acted on those "talents and abilities". He helped with the crowds, healed the sick, gave of Himself so others would know God, and regularly communed with God. He had twelve people in His small group, known as the disciples, with whom He told parables and shared what was going to happen in the future. In the garden, the night of his betrayal, Jesus said to Peter, James, and John in Matthew 26:38, "My soul is deeply grieved, to the point of death; remain here and keep watch with Me." Although they understood Jesus was deeply troubled when He asked for help, they let

Him down three times by falling asleep and not praying. He implored them, "So, you men could not keep watch with Me for one hour? Keep watching and praying that you may not enter into temptation; the spirit is willing, but the flesh is weak" (Matthew 26:40b-41). Three of the closest men who knew Jesus personally let Jesus down and Jesus still loved them.

We know transparency with God is about a relationship and communication. Similarly, transparency with others is about our relationship with them and open communication. We have to include others in our journey to transparency. God created us for communion and fellowship with Him and others. Even Jesus knew the significance of praying as he shared His journey and ministry with the disciples. Still, they betrayed Him, let Him down, and denied Him. Nevertheless, He showed them love and chose to walk alongside them. With this being the case, why wouldn't we follow suit with Him and have relationships with others? Sin in our world not only affects us, but our relationship with others.

We use our selfishness and many others reasons as an excuse to build walls around us for protection. In reality, the only thing to protect us is love. This is a love that can only come from an active relationship with God. It cannot be stagnate or warm. We must be on fire for God in our lives for there to be a hope of true transparency with others. At this point in our lives, we will be close enough with God to know what we can safely share and with whom. We will be able to see others as God sees them just as Jesus saw Peter as the "rock of His church" and not the one who denied Him. Prayer is vital to our transparency. Just as Adam and Eve walked in the garden and communed with God because their relationship with God was right and good, we, too, can walk and commune with God through our prayers. Yes, trust will be broken because of sin at some point, but we must end the cycle of sin by asking for forgiveness and giving forgiveness. Sin hinders our relationship with others and teaches us to hide from others because of hurts and mistrust. We must not allow transparency to stop. Instead, we must tear off the masks and tear down the walls through our love and prayer. Let's begin to see others as God sees them and treat them how we would want to be treated. This journey of tearing off our clothes, or walls, and becoming open, vulnerable, and transparent with each other, must begin with us and our relationship with God.

## *Questions*

1. Is your first feeling about being transparent with others positive or negative? Why?

2. How have your interactions of being transparent affected you in your transparency journey?

3. What is the hardest part for you in admitting to others that you are struggling?

4. How does selfishness inhibit transparency for you?

5. Who has murdered your reputation and how? Did you surrender, give up, decide they can't define your life, or are you still fighting back?

6. Do you struggle with perfection? If so, how has this affected your transparency with others?

7. How do you trust others when they have broken your trust?

8. Does pride and self-reliance go hand-in-hand for you or are they two different issues?

9. What impact has materialism had on your life? Do you say it impacts your transparency with others in a positive or negative way?

10. How has your prayer life impacted your ability to be transparent with others?

## Group Transparency Exercise:

Have each member of your group tell which area they struggle with the most in being transparent with others: selfishness, embarrassment, vulnerability, perfectionism, showing weaknesses/pride, trust, losing privacy, self-reliance, materialism/comparing ourselves to others. After the area is shared, have each member address how it has negatively affected them in being transparent with others.

*Chapter 6*

# Transparency with Love

Transparency is a murky, dangerous, exciting ride in our Christian life. Our experiences of being transparent vary vastly and are based upon our personal circumstances, where we are in our relationship with God, and our relationships with others. We all start at different levels of transparency due to past hurts and trust issues both of which tend to hold us back on our adventure. It is up to us to have the courage to embark upon a journey that will frighten us, cause us pain, bring tears of joy, and bond us together in love. That's what this transparency thing is all about: learning to love enough to let go of ourselves. In this way, we let God have our lives, we give our lives to others, and we join with others on their journey of life.

Our discussions in the previous chapters have helped advance our talk and understanding of transparency. This understanding does not necessarily make it easier to begin; however, begin we must. We approach our journey cautiously as one walking into a dark room. We are careful to feel around to make sure we will not hit anything or get hurt. Likewise, in our lives, we put out our arms to keep others at a safe distance, as they do with us. If our desire is to wrap our arms around each other in a comforting and protective manner, we must act now, and turn on the light of transparency in our lives so others may see God and not worry about walking in the darkness. In this manner of transparency, true love can be found.

Love is a peculiar word that brings up many different emotions as does transparency. We began our discussion of transparency by defining what it really means. As we compare the relationship of transparency and love, we must turn to the Bible for our definition. Most people know the biblical definition of love from 1 Corinthians 13. Take just a moment and read it out loud, so you can verbally hear the words in a new, fresh way.

> *"If I speak with the tongues of men and of angels, but do not have love, I have become a noisy gong or a clanging cymbal. If I have the gift of prophecy, and know all mysteries and all knowledge; and if I have all faith, so as to remove mountains, but do not have love, I am nothing. And if I give all my possessions to feed the poor, and if I surrender my body to be burned, but do not have love, it profits me nothing. Love is patient, love is kind and is not jealous; love does not brag and is not arrogant, does not act unbecomingly; it does not seek its own, is not provoked, does not take into account a wrong suffered, does not rejoice in unrighteousness, but rejoices with the truth; bears all things, believes all things, hopes all things, endures all things. Love never fails; but if there are gifts of*

*prophecy, they will be done away; if there are tongues, they will cease; if there is knowledge, it will be done away. For we know in part and we prophesy in part; but when the perfect comes, the partial will be done away. When I was a child, I used to speak like a child, think like a child, reason like a child; when I became a man, I did away with childish things. For now we see in a mirror dimly, but then face to face; now I know in part, but then I will know fully just as I also have been fully known. But now faith, hope, love, abide these three; but the greatest of these is love.*

Paul described love to the Corinthians in this letter by his honest assessment of where they were in life: in a mess. We discussed earlier how Paul wrote this letter to the Christians in Corinth because they had become worldly and distracted in their walk with God. It was hard to tell the church people from the non-church people; yet, Paul tells us about love and how we, as Christian believers, are supposed to live. Paul might as well be writing this letter to our culture today for we are, in fact, in a mess. He starts out by setting the record straight and telling us that without love we are nothing. Nothing matters if we do everything right, say all the right things, or do all the right deeds; love is an absolute. He then goes on to describe what love is and what love is not. As he writes about this love, Paul shows us how love can empower us to be transparent. The very first attributes Paul points out are: "love is patient, love is kind, it is not jealous".

Since we started our transparency journey with Jim and Mary, we will complete the circle and end our story with them as our examples. Mary was hurting and struggling to know who she was as a person. Her group patiently listened to her and cared for her emotional needs as she became transparent with them about her struggles. Because of their actions of being patient and the love they displayed,

Mary was able to effectively share her life and circumstances with them and ultimately found Jesus.

Jim knew there was love from his small group because each week they took time to share from their hearts the "big" burdens they carried. He knew he could count on his group to support him in these big things. Because Jim appreciated these men so much though, he didn't want to burden them with the small things in his life. He didn't know how to be transparent and how to ask for help with the small things when there were many others in life simply struggling to survive. Jim did pretty well for himself and if he were to ask for help in these small areas, he wondered if it would be considered bragging. Paul adamantly states that love does not brag, and is not arrogant! What was Jim to do? Overall, there was not much to complain about in his life; in fact, he felt pretty blessed. How could he be transparent and express these inconveniences without sounding arrogant?

Mary, on the other hand, was struggling so much with her daughter that if she could get help from anyone, she would take the help. This freedom and love she felt from her group allowed her to share both her small and big things in life; most revolving around her daughter, June. There was not much she had to brag about in her life because she felt her love towards her daughter was unbecoming; it was wrong.

In her human attempt to survive as a single parent, every circumstance and every issue in her life felt like it must be dealt with immediately. Her first reaction, before she accepted Jesus in her life, was always based on how it would affect her and not how Jesus desired for her to act. Paul described this as "seeking its own". She still struggled to react in the proper way each time, but as her relationship with God continued to grow, she was starting to think twice before reacting, thanks to the love the group showed her.

Mary's love towards herself, God, and others continued to grow the more she felt her group's love and support. This transparency with them also allowed her to see the times she provoked her daughter. June had a tendency to make her so mad, and Mary's first reaction was to find a way to make June just as angry. She realized how flawed this love was and began to hold her tongue during the times she and June would fight. When June wouldn't come home on time, would lie to Mary's face, or would say hurtful words to her, Mary realized she couldn't hold these hurts inside of her. With the help of her group, she felt safe being transparent and was able to talk through these hurts. The hurts didn't magically go away, but Mary was able to realize it was necessary for her to pray for June, as well as herself, during these times. After all, just a few months ago, Mary had been just like June.

Jim didn't really understand the issues of those like Mary. He grew up in a Christian home and knew what love was supposed to look like. It had not always been perfect; yet, love was modeled in such a way for him that he always felt loved and accepted. He had never been overly hurt by anyone, nor really felt the sting of rejection that cut him to the core. True love was more of a normal thing than hatred, rejection, and betrayal. He appreciated how those like Mary were able to overcome their previous lives and live the new life of Christ. He welcomed the openness of others as they would embark on a new journey with Christ. His journey, for as long as he could remember, though, had always included Christ.

Still, in Jim's mind, if situations that had happened to Mary would have occurred in his life, he wondered if he would be able to be transparent, or how much he would handle it on his own or in a better way. Jim grew up in a Christian home and now has a Christian family of his own. He "does not rejoice in unrighteousness, but rejoices with the truth." He does not like the evil in this world and struggles with why good things happen to bad people, as well as why bad things happen to good people. Jim has nothing against someone like Mary. He truly desires for them to know the truth and love he has known his entire life. The problem he has is in his inability to relate to others who are not like him. He does not know how to effectively love them. Even within his group, Jim knows there are those who perceive his life as perfect, so he feels incapable of addressing the small items with them.

One thing Jim has forgotten is that by admitting our shortcomings with others we actually provide them hope; hope that they are not alone when their life is far from perfect. When we open up about our struggles, we provide them a light at the end of their present-day tunnel to know they don't walk alone. Our Christian walk will have its ups and downs because this world is fallen. As we admit there are areas where we struggle, like Mary did with her group, we become transparent so others realize this seemingly perfect life still has issues. This transparency will further break things down for us to realize no matter how big or small the issue we face, it all comes down to our trying to handle it on our own apart from God. Our circumstances vary from one person to another, as with Jim and Mary, but all circumstances are still issues or problems we face in life and we must decide how much of these issues we will choose to disclose to others.

Paul states, love "bears all things, believes all things, hopes all things, endures all things." Mary was able to admit to others her problems with her daughter. The love from the group helped her to bear her burdens. They gave her hope that she could get through this time in her life and they enabled her to endure her struggles. Her life was far from perfect; still, she learned to lean on others and become transparent with them, because of the love they showed her. Although it appears Jim has a perfect life and a pretty good understanding of love, he is still coming up short. Whether it's due to his self-reliance, his fear of letting others into his life, or the fear of losing control, he is not allowing others to help him "bear all things".

Paul's last statement that "love never fails" hits Jim in a funny way. He feels incapable of letting go of the small things in his life. It was easier for Mary to let go and be transparent with her group because she had nowhere to go but up. Jim, on the other hand, feels he has nowhere to go but down if he were to open up and be truly transparent. He is finding his pride is creeping back into his situation as he is used to taking care of himself and so many others. If "love never fails" and he is unwilling to venture out on the small things, does this mean he does not truly trust "love" itself; whether that of God or others?

Our reading of 1Corinthians 13, in regards to the life of Jim and Mary, has highlighted some life experiences we deal with daily and compared them to this Scripture. There is one more passage we need to explore on the topic of love before we end our time together. This passage explores why we should love, as well as the true origin of our love. It equips the "Jims" of this world with the reason for opening up to others when he feels defeated, embarrassed, or undeserving. Let's read 1 John 4:7-12:

> "Beloved, let us love one another, for love is from God; and everyone who loves is born of God and knows God. The one who does not love does not know God, for God is love. By this the love of God was manifested in us, that God has sent His only begotten Son into the world so that we might live through Him. In this love, not that we loved God, but that He loved us and sent His Son to be the propitiation for our sins. Beloved, if God so loved us, we also ought to love one another. No one has seen God at any time; if we love one another, God abides in us, and His love is perfected in us."

You see, at the core, love is not about us at all; it is about God. It is His very nature and His very being. We have not seen God face to face on this earth. Yet, Paul says in verse 12, "if we love one another, God abides in us, and His love is perfected in us". Mary never opened up until she felt the love and support from those around her in her small group. This group took on the form of God through their love and Mary felt and saw that love in action. She wasn't looking at the lives of those around her; she was looking at the love of God through them. This love gave her the courage to be transparent, and through this transparency she found God.

We must be careful when we expect the love of God to be the same as the love we have in our world. In fact, the perception is usually on different spectrums. The perception of the world and society as a loveless place, and the interpretation of love in terms of individual emotion, not to mention erotic attraction, stand over against the message that is the gospel (Smith 1991, 111). The message of the gospel is love. The requirements and expectations we have of love are often based on our experiences in life, when, in fact, they should be based on God and His sending of His Son. "The very definition of love turns upon God's sending, i.e., giving up, his Son for the expiation (the act of making atonement) of sins...because Jesus deals with and does away with sin, we live through him...Particularly important is the fact that God has taken the initiative. The definition of love proceeds from God; 'not that we loved God but that he loved us'" (107).

If we are to truly understand God's love, we must realize He loved us first. His love is far superior to the love we are capable of exhibiting, and there are no works we can do to make Him love us any more or any less. He loves us unconditionally just for being us; being us in both big and small circumstances. This acceptance of God's love gives us the confidence of an unending love that can only be shared and not locked away. This love that is shared in God's ways allows us to be more trusting of others and more transparent with them when we know their foundation of love is based upon God's love and not that of this world. "Moreover, it is God's love for us that defines what true love requires, which is the commitment to sacrifice one's most beloved possession for another's gain. So for God, love required that he send 'his Son as an atoning sacrifice for our sins'" (Gaebelein 1981, 12:343).

True love required Mary to open up to others about her problems with her daughter. Jim had limited love to the big things of his life. True love required him to give up his self-reliance, pride, and his expectations that he didn't need to bother others with his small and simple issues. This true love required him to admit *to himself* that these small issues weren't really silly. Maybe Jim felt he shouldn't ask God to help him with the small things because in his mind God had already blessed him with a great life. Perhaps Jim was too ashamed to admit his issues to others because he had once judged others when he felt they should have handled their life's situations better.

When it comes down to it, though, he is ashamed to admit he knows how those like Mary feel: discontent, alone, hopeless. With a pang in his gut and a brokenness of his heart, Jim realized *he* is "Mary" before she decided to open up her life. He, like Mary, must take the plunge and simply open up when prompted by the Holy Spirit. He will have to give himself permission to not be the strong one and allow God to be the strong one of his life.

We serve a God who is over us and all of our circumstances; whether we relate better to Jim or Mary. He loves us more than we can ever imagine. God desires for us to be transparent with ourselves, Him and others. We need to remember God loved us first. Our love for Him is not based on rules, regulations, or religion; it is based on Him giving us love and our response of an open, honest, loyal, and transparent relationship with Him. Through our relationship with Him we can more clearly absorb His love into our lives. When we spend more time with Him, we will experience His love in our lives, and His love will be interwoven into our thoughts, actions, and attitudes as we realize who He is and who we are in Him.

As our relationship deepens with God daily, our very nature and desires will change. This change will enable us to open our hearts and lives to others around us and to be transparent with them, as God desires. He will guide us to those with whom we need to share. He will prepare those we are to encounter as we pray for those we will encounter. "Insofar as we love one another, God abides in us and his love is perfected, in the sense of completed, in us. God's love is then brought to perfection or completion in us to the extent that we love our fellow believers" (Smith 1991, 110).

Verse eleven states, "Beloved, if God so loved us, we also ought to love one another." "The author continues to show that the true nature of love is unselfish and sacrificial. In 3:16 he appealed to Jesus, who laid down his life for his brothers, as the example for believers to follow. Now he directs attention to God's own example: 'Since God so loved us, we also ought to love one another.' The nature of the argument is not properly deductive but analogical... 'If the children of God must be holy because He is holy...and merciful because He is merciful, so they must be loving because He is loving – not with the 'must' of external compulsion but with the 'must' of inward constraint: God's love is poured into their hearts by the Holy Spirit whom they have received'" (Gaebelein 1981,12:343).

First John 4:21 ends the chapter with a commandment: "that the one who loves God should love his brother also". John simply rephrases verse 11 for the readers, in case we missed it earlier, that loving others is not an option if we desire to belong to God. Without love for God, we do not really have His nature inside us and we are not of Him. Yes, there will be people who will turn our words around and hurt us because there is evil in the world. Yet, how will this hurting world ever see God's love if we are not willing to be transparent and share what God is actively doing in our lives?

We are all on a journey here on earth and transparency is hard. We do not slow down enough in life to know others, God, or even ourselves very well. But, now is the time to slow down. Now is the time to move forward in this transparency journey in love: in God's love. We must take the first step across the bridge of transparency. This means we will be out over troubled waters, at times, and others will be able to see us from both sides of the land. We will feel alone, exposed, rejected, and loved; possibly all at the same time. One bridge of transparency might be a small bridge and other bridges might be like the Chesapeake Bay Bridge going both over and under water for miles. Regardless, God has already paid the toll for us to cross the bridge when He sent His Son to die for our sins. He gave up His most priceless treasure for our benefit.

Now is the time for us to give up our most priceless treasure for the benefit of others: *ourselves* God will lead us where we need to go and will direct our paths as we allow Him to guide us. Yes, transparency is hard. It is a matter of prayer, introspection, relationship, and love. We are commanded to love others because God loves us. First John 5:3 states, "For this is the love of God, that we keep His commandments; and His commandments are not burdensome." God never gives us more than we can handle. He gave up His Son for us. What are we willing to give up for God today? Let's embark on the road to transparency...in God's love!

## *Questions:*

1.  Do non-church people have a hard time seeing you as a Christian? If so, what areas of your life need to better resemble that of Christ?

2.  What aspect of transparency needs the most work in your life? With yourself? Expectations? God? Others? Name one way you plan to address this issue in the next week.

3.  According to Paul's definition of love in 1 Corinthians 13:4–8a, which area of love is easiest for you and why? Which area is the hardest?

4.  True love is modeled after God's love. How do you define true love and how does this definition compare to God's love in 1 John 4?

5.  What is your most beloved possession? Are you ready to commit to sacrifice your most beloved possession for another's gain, as God did by sending Jesus to earth?

6. We discussed transparency with yourself, mental expectations, physical expectations, God, and others. Are you more like Jim or Mary in each of these areas and in which area do you struggle the most?

7. Was there a turning point in your life that skewed the way you looked at love? Did this affect your relationship with God and your view of His love for you?

8. Has your view of transparency changed positively or negatively while working through this book and why?

### Group Transparency Exercise:

Have each member in your group share an area of their lives that most resembles that of the world. After they give an example, have them decide which part of Paul's definition of love would help them bring this area closer to being like God and not like the world.

# References

Bonhoeffer, Dietrich. *Life Together.* New York: Harper & Row, Publishers, Inc., 1954.

Gaebelein, Frank E., ed. *The Expositor's Bible Commentary.* Vol. 5, *Psalms,* by Willem A. VanGemeren. Grand Rapids: Zondervan Publishing House, 1991.

_____. *The Expositor's Bible Commentary.* Vol. 8, *Matthew,* by D. A. Carson. Grand Rapids: Zondervan Publishing House, 1984.

_____. *The Expositor's Bible Commentary.* Vol. 12, *1, 2, 3 John,* by Clonn W. Barker Grand Rapids: Zondervan Publishing House, 1981.

*Merriam-Webster's Dictionary of English Usage.* Springfield, MA: Merriam-Webster, 1994.

Smith, D. Moody. *Interpretation: A Bible Commentary for Teaching and Preaching, First, Second, and Third John. Louisville: John Knox Press, 1991.*

Steven Kalas, "It's Easy to Ruin a Person's Reputation", *Las Vegas Review-Journal,* February 28, 2012.

www.ingramcontent.com/pod-product-compliance
Lightning Source LLC
Chambersburg PA
CBHW060308050426
42448CB00009B/1760